NORTHERN ITALY

Travel Guide 2025

Practical Tips, Key Destinations, Activities, and Local Insights for Your Journey in Milan, Venice, Florence, and Beyond

Alexandra R. Meyer

Disclaimer

The information contained in this book is for educational and informational purposes only. The author and publisher are not liable for any damages arising from the use or misuse of the information provided. The content is based on the author's knowledge, experience, and research at the time of publication. It should not be considered as legal, financial, medical, or other professional advice. Always consult a qualified professional before making decisions that could affect your

well-being or that of others.

Travel information, including prices, schedules, and offerings may be subject to changes.

TABLE OF CONTENT

Chapter 1: Welcome to Northern Italy – A Journey Through Elegance and Culture

Northern Italy is a realm where timeless elegance meets a vibrant cultural tapestry, inviting travelers to discover a world of breathtaking landscapes, architectural marvels, and culinary treasures. From the snow-capped peaks of the Dolomites to the shimmering shores of Lake Como, every corner of this enchanting region tells a story of sophistication and charm.

Wander through the fashion capital of Milan, where innovation meets tradition in both couture and cuisine. Explore the romantic waterways of Venice, a city built on dreams, or lose yourself in the Renaissance brilliance of Florence's northern neighbor, Verona. Beyond the iconic cities, Northern Italy's hidden gems beckon—medieval villages perched on hilltops, sprawling vineyards of Piedmont, and tranquil coastal retreats along Liguria's famed Riviera.

The region's gastronomy is as diverse as its landscapes, with creamy risottos, rich truffle-infused dishes, and sparkling wines to indulge your senses. Art lovers will marvel at the works of masters like Leonardo da Vinci, while history enthusiasts can trace the footsteps of emperors and poets.

Whether you seek adventure, romance, or cultural immersion, Northern Italy promises an unforgettable journey. Let its elegance, history, and warmth capture your heart—welcome to a place where every moment is a masterpiece

Why Northern Italy Captivates Every Traveler

Northern Italy has a way of enchanting visitors, drawing them into its world of beauty, history, and flavor. It's a region that speaks to the heart with its timeless appeal, leaving unforgettable memories. Here are eight reasons why it continues to attract travelers from all over:

1. **Architectural Treasures:** From the Gothic spires of Milan's Duomo to the Renaissance charm of Verona's amphitheater, Northern Italy showcases some of Europe's most breathtaking buildings. Every corner tells a story that connects you to the past.
2. **Culinary Excellence:** This region is home to globally loved dishes like risotto, prosciutto, and balsamic vinegar. Each meal reflects the land's traditions, making every bite a journey through Italian heritage.
3. **The Majesty of the Alps:** The snow-capped peaks of the Alps offer a spectacular backdrop for activities like skiing, hiking, or simply soaking in the views. Nature's grandeur feels limitless here.
4. **Romantic Waterways of Venice:** There's no experience quite like gliding through Venice's canals, where gondolas float past historic palaces and bridges. The city's ambiance is unlike any other.
5. **Art and Innovation:** Home to the works of Leonardo da Vinci and countless other visionaries, Northern Italy brims with creativity, blending old masterpieces with modern marvels.
6. **Wine Heaven:** Regions like Piedmont and Veneto produce some of the world's finest wines. Sampling a glass of Barolo or Prosecco in its birthplace is a sensory experience to treasure.
7. **Lake District Serenity:** Lakes Garda, Como, and Maggiore are perfect for tranquil getaways, framed by picturesque villages and serene waters.

8. **Historic Towns and Cities:** From Bologna's ancient streets to Turin's regal squares, Northern Italy showcases a variety of cities where culture and history thrive.

An Overview: Geography, Climate, and Regional Diversity

Northern Italy stands as a captivating mosaic of geographical contrasts, from towering mountains to serene lakes, rolling hills to vibrant cities. This region, with its distinct landscapes and climates, is a fascinating area that offers an array of experiences, whether you are wandering through the alpine heights or soaking in the Mediterranean warmth.

Geographically, Northern Italy is defined by its proximity to several key features that shape both its climate and lifestyle. The Alps form a dramatic northern boundary, their snow-capped peaks offering not only a scenic backdrop but also a playground for winter sports enthusiasts. These mountains create a natural barrier, affecting the climate and weather patterns that sweep through the region. To the south of the Alps, you encounter the Po River, Italy's longest river, which flows across the fertile plains and serves as the lifeblood of agriculture and trade.

The Po Valley, also known as the Pianura Padana, stretches across much of Northern Italy, offering rich, flat terrain that is perfect for farming. This area benefits from a temperate climate, characterized by hot summers and cold, foggy winters, which gives the land its agricultural prowess. This is where you'll find Italy's most productive farming regions, supplying the country with grains, rice, and vegetables, and creating a backdrop of green fields stretching for miles.

In contrast, the northernmost areas of Italy, particularly in regions like Trentino-Alto Adige, are dominated by the imposing peaks of the Alps. Here, the climate is markedly cooler, and the landscape is dotted with alpine meadows, glacial lakes, and dense forests. This part of Italy is a paradise for nature lovers, hikers, and outdoor enthusiasts. In winter, it transforms into a hub for skiing and snowboarding, while in summer, it offers hiking trails that lead to breathtaking panoramic views of the valleys below.

Moving closer to the Mediterranean coast, the climate gradually shifts to milder, more temperate conditions. The regions of Liguria and Emilia-Romagna, for example, enjoy a climate that allows for a lush, Mediterranean lifestyle. The weather is often warm and sunny, ideal for producing some of Italy's most famous food products, from olive oil in Liguria to the famed Parma ham in Emilia-Romagna. These coastal areas also boast charming seaside villages, stunning beaches, and a slower pace of life, making them popular spots for both locals and travelers seeking tranquility.

The regional diversity of Northern Italy is not just confined to geography and climate; it also extends to the cultures and languages spoken. In some areas, such as the Aosta Valley and Trentino-Alto Adige, German is spoken alongside Italian, reflecting the historic influences of neighboring countries. The food varies significantly as well, with hearty alpine dishes like polenta and speck in the north, shifting to lighter seafood-based cuisine along the Ligurian coast. Each region within Northern Italy contributes its own distinct flavors, traditions, and characteristics to the larger cultural fabric of the country.

Whether you are planning to explore the cultural riches of cities like Milan and Venice, trek through the dramatic mountain landscapes, or relax by the shores of Italy's beautiful lakes, Northern Italy offers an abundance of opportunities. Its rich geography, diverse climate, and varied regional flavors create a region that is always changing yet consistently full of surprises. Northern Italy is a place that never fails to captivate, whether through its landscapes, history, or welcoming people.

Key Factors:

1. **Geographical contrasts**: From the Alps to the Po Valley, Northern Italy's landscape is marked by variety.

2. **Climate**: A blend of alpine cold in the north and Mediterranean warmth in the south, influencing local life.

3. **Cultural diversity**: Languages and traditions that reflect the region's complex history.

4. **Agricultural richness**: The Po Valley's fertile plains and the food products that thrive there.

5. **Tourism potential**: Ski resorts in the Alps, lakeside retreats, and vibrant cities all offer unique experiences.

A Glimpse into Northern Italy's History and Traditions

Northern Italy weaves together a rich history and vibrant traditions that echo through its ancient streets and picturesque landscapes. This region, steeped in centuries of cultural evolution, invites you to explore its intricate past and enduring customs. From the grand architecture of Renaissance cities like Florence and Milan to the rustic charm of rural villages, Northern Italy is a mosaic of historical influences and local life.

The legacy of the Roman Empire is ever-present in its ruins and roads, while the elegance of medieval and Renaissance eras lives on in the region's castles, palaces, and cathedrals. Northern Italy's history is not merely confined to its architecture—it's alive in the vibrant festivals, folk music, and time-honored crafts that have been passed down through generations.

Traditions here are closely tied to the land. The region boasts culinary practices rooted in local produce, from creamy risottos of Lombardy to the delicate wines of Piedmont. Family-run trattorias serve recipes perfected over centuries, giving visitors a taste of authenticity on every plate.

The people of Northern Italy take pride in their heritage, evident in the passionate preservation of dialects, artisan techniques, and community celebrations. Whether strolling through the canals of Venice or admiring the Dolomites, you'll sense a deep connection between the land and its inhabitants.

For travelers, Northern Italy presents not just a chance to see historical landmarks but to feel the soul of a region that thrives on blending its storied past with its lively present. Each corner holds a story, each tradition a glimpse into a way of life that remains as captivating today as it was centuries ago.

Best Times to Visit: Seasonal Charm, Festivals, and Events

Northern Italy is a region that surprises and delights in every season. From the snow-capped Alps to the sunlit canals of Venice, the area offers a mix of cultural, historical, and natural attractions that change with the seasons. Each time of year brings its own special atmosphere, weather, and opportunities for exploration, making it important to plan your trip according to what you want to experience. Here's a breakdown of the best times to visit, including the weather, key activities, and notable festivals and events.

Spring (March to May): A Time of Renewal

Spring in Northern Italy is marked by mild temperatures, blossoming flowers, and vibrant landscapes. The days gradually lengthen, and the region starts to wake from the winter chill. March is still cool, but by May, the weather is comfortably warm, making it ideal for outdoor activities.

Weather Considerations: Temperatures in spring vary from 10°C (50°F) in March to 20°C (68°F) in May, with evenings still cool, especially in the mountains.

Activities: Spring is perfect for hiking in the Dolomites or exploring the lakes, such as Lake Como and Lake Garda, where the surrounding hills and gardens begin to bloom. The vineyards in the Langhe region also come alive, with opportunities for early wine-tasting tours.

Festivals & Events:

- **Milan Design Week (April):** A global event for design lovers, Milan comes alive with innovative exhibitions and installations.

- **Verona Opera Festival (April-May):** Held in the iconic Arena di Verona, this festival is a highlight for opera enthusiasts.

Summer (June to August): Vibrant and Lively

Summer is the high season in Northern Italy, bringing long, sunny days and bustling cities. The weather is hot, particularly in cities like Milan and Turin, where temperatures can reach 30°C (86°F) or higher. However, the alpine regions remain cooler, offering an escape from the heat.

Weather Considerations: Expect warm, sunny days with temperatures ranging from 25°C (77°F) in the lowlands to 15°C (59°F) in the mountains. It's a great time for outdoor adventures, but be prepared for occasional summer thunderstorms.

Activities: The summer months are ideal for outdoor exploration. Go cycling through the vineyards of Piedmont, take a boat ride on Lake Como, or explore the charming towns of the Italian Riviera. For those seeking beach time, the coastal areas of Liguria and Friuli Venezia Giulia offer relaxing escapes.

Festivals & Events:

- **La Palio di Siena (July-August):** While technically not in Northern Italy, this historic horse race in Siena is an iconic event close enough to consider for a summer trip.

- **Venice Film Festival (August-September):** A glamorous event that attracts celebrities from around the world, making it a key part of Venice's summer scene.

Autumn (September to November): Harvest Time and Cozy Vibes

Autumn brings cooler temperatures and a more peaceful atmosphere to Northern Italy. As the summer crowds dissipate, the region embraces the harvest season, with vineyards full of ripe grapes and chestnut trees shedding their leaves. This is the time for cozy sweater weather and exploring local markets.

Weather Considerations: Expect cooler temperatures, ranging from 12°C (54°F) in the Alps to 22°C (72°F) in the cities. The weather is usually crisp and clear, making it ideal for sightseeing without the summer heat.

Activities: Autumn is the perfect time to explore the region's rich culinary offerings. From truffle hunting in Alba to attending harvest festivals, this is a season that celebrates food and drink. Hiking is also exceptional during this time, with the fall foliage offering breathtaking views of the mountains and lakes.

Festivals & Events:

- **Truffle Festival (October):** Held in Alba, this event is a must for food lovers, offering tastings and truffle-themed activities.

- **Venice International Film Festival (September):** For those interested in cinema, Venice becomes a cultural hotspot during this prestigious festival.

Winter (December to February): A Magical Season for Snow and History

Winter in Northern Italy is all about snow, cozy villages, and the magical atmosphere of the holidays. The mountains are a haven for skiers, while cities like Milan, Venice, and Verona become enchanting places with festive decorations and Christmas markets.

Weather Considerations: The temperatures can drop to around 0°C (32°F) in the cities, while the mountains experience colder weather with snowfall. Winter sports enthusiasts flock to the Alps for skiing and snowboarding.

Activities: Whether you're skiing in the Dolomites or exploring the Christmas markets in Bolzano, winter offers plenty of outdoor and cultural experiences. Venice's winter mist and Milan's seasonal shopping sales make the cities even more captivating.

Festivals & Events:

- **Milan Fashion Week (February):** A must-see for fashion aficionados, Milan's Fashion Week is one of the most anticipated events in the fashion world.

- **Venice Carnival (February):** With its elaborate masks and costumes, this world-renowned carnival is one of Italy's most famous winter events.

Whether you're hiking through the snow-capped mountains, exploring vibrant cities, or attending one of the many local festivals, there's always something to look forward to throughout the year. By choosing the right time to visit based on your interests and the experiences you're after, you'll be able to make the most of this beautiful region, no matter the season.

Budgeting and Expenses

- **Accommodation**: From €50 for budget stays to €300+ for luxury hotels.
- **Meals**: Casual meals start at €10–€20, while fine dining can range between €50–€100+ per person.
- **Transport**: Train tickets range from €10–€50 depending on the distance. Local buses cost around €1.50 per ride.
- **Activities**: Museum entries cost around €10–€20, while guided tours can be €50+.
- **Tips**: Carry cash for smaller vendors, but credit cards are widely accepted.

Local Laws and Regulations

- **Tipping**: Not mandatory but appreciated for good service. Round up to the nearest euro at cafes and restaurants.

- **Smoking**: Prohibited indoors and in public spaces like train stations.
- **Alcohol**: Drinking in public spaces is restricted in certain areas; check local signs.
- **Traffic Rules**: Follow speed limits (50 km/h in towns, 130 km/h on highways). Watch for ZTL (limited traffic zones) in historic centers to avoid fines.
- **Cultural Norms**: Dress modestly when visiting churches and religious sites.

Explore Northern Italy with Ease: Scan the Travel Map Code!

Discover Northern Italy effortlessly! Scan the QR code in this guide to unlock your interactive map, featuring iconic cities like Milan and Venice, picturesque lakes, scenic mountain roads, and the best spots to savor authentic Italian cuisine and culture.

How to Use It?

1. Open your phone's camera or QR scanner.

2. Scan the code.

3. Access your personalized guide instantly, no downloads needed!

Navigate Northern Italy like a local and uncover every hidden gem, from the medieval charm of Verona to the rolling hills of Tuscany, with just one scan. Your Italian adventure begins now!

Chapter 2: Planning Your Perfect Northern Italy Trip

Planning a trip to Northern Italy is about preparing for an adventure through breathtaking landscapes, cultural treasures, and vibrant cities. This chapter will guide you step by step—from sorting travel documents to choosing the best transportation and saving on costs, helping you enjoy the journey with ease and excitement.

Entry Essentials: Visas, Travel Documents, and Tips for Visitors

Planning a trip to Northern Italy? The first step toward a smooth, worry-free journey is understanding the visa requirements and preparing the necessary travel documents. This comprehensive guide will help you navigate the entry process with ease and confidence.

Who Needs a Visa to Visit Northern Italy?

As part of the Schengen Area, Northern Italy follows the visa policies of 26 other European countries. Whether you need a visa depends on your nationality and the purpose of your visit.

- **Visa-Free Access:** Citizens of the European Union (EU), European Economic Area (EEA), and Switzerland can enter Northern Italy with a valid passport or national ID card. Visitors from countries like the United States, Canada, Australia, New Zealand, Japan, and South Korea are granted visa-free stays of up to 90 days within a 180-day period for tourism, business, or family visits.

- **Visa Requirement:** If your country is not on the visa-waiver list, you'll need to apply for a Schengen visa before traveling to

Northern Italy. This applies to travelers from nations such as India, China, Nigeria, and South Africa.

Types of Visas Available

Depending on your travel purpose, there are several visa categories to choose from:

- **Tourist Visa (Schengen Visa Type C):** For short stays (up to 90 days), including tourism, family visits, or business trips.

- **Business Visa:** For professionals attending conferences, meetings, or other work-related events.

- **Student Visa (Schengen Visa Type D):** For academic programs longer than 90 days.

- **Family or Dependent Visa:** For individuals joining family members who are already residing in Northern Italy.

- **Work Visa:** Required for those planning to take up paid employment in Italy.

Applying for a Tourist Visa

If you need a visa to visit Northern Italy, it's important to apply in advance. Here's a step-by-step breakdown of the process:

Step-by-Step Application Process

1. **Determine Your Visa Type:** Identify the appropriate visa category based on your purpose of travel.

2. **Complete the Application Form:** Fill out the Schengen visa application form online or download it from the official website: https://vistoperitalia.esteri.it.

3. **Schedule an Appointment:** Book a visa appointment at the Italian consulate or visa application center in your country.

4. **Prepare Supporting Documents:** Gather all necessary documents (outlined below).

5. **Attend the Appointment:** Submit your application, provide biometric data (fingerprints), and pay the application fee.

6. **Wait for Processing:** Visa processing generally takes 15 days, but it may take longer during busy periods.

Required Documents and Fees

- A completed Schengen visa application form

- A valid passport (with at least two blank pages and validity extending three months beyond your intended stay)

- Two passport-sized photos

- Proof of travel insurance (covering at least €30,000)

- Round-trip flight reservations or travel itinerary

- Proof of accommodation (hotel bookings, rental agreements, or invitation letters)

- Proof of sufficient financial means (bank statements, payslips, or sponsorship letters)

- Visa fee: €80 for adults; reduced fees for children and specific applicants.

How to Apply Online

To begin your visa application process, visit the official Italian Visa Application Website: https://vistoperitalia.esteri.it. This portal allows you to complete forms, upload documents, and schedule appointments easily.

Applying Through a Consulate or Embassy

Alternatively, you can submit your application in person at the nearest Italian consulate or embassy. For a list of consulates worldwide, visit Italy's Ministry of Foreign Affairs: https://www.esteri.it/mae/en/.

Family and Dependent Visas

If you're joining family members residing in Northern Italy, you can apply for a family reunification visa.

Eligibility for Family Visas

You may apply for a family visa if you are a spouse, child under 18, dependent parent, or unmarried partner of an Italian resident or citizen. Proof of your relationship is required.

Required Documents and Application Steps

- A completed visa application form

- A valid passport

- Proof of relationship (e.g., marriage certificate, birth certificate)

- Sponsor's residence permit or Italian ID

- Proof of accommodation in Italy

- Visa fee: €116

Submit your application to the Italian consulate or visa center in your country. Processing times may vary.

Visa Extensions and Renewals

If you want to extend your stay in Northern Italy, you must apply for an extension before your visa expires.

How to Extend Your Stay

- Submit a request to the local immigration office (Questura) where you are staying.

- Provide valid reasons, such as unforeseen circumstances or ongoing medical treatment.

Renewal Procedures and Requirements

Extensions are rarely granted for tourist visas unless in exceptional circumstances. For long-term visas, the renewal process requires:

- A valid reason for extending your stay

- Updated supporting documents

- Renewal fee: €30–€50

Overstaying Your Visa: Consequences and Penalties

Overstaying your visa can result in fines, travel bans, or future visa denials. To avoid these consequences, always adhere to your visa's expiration date or apply for an extension in advance.

- **Travel Insurance**: Always carry valid travel insurance to cover medical emergencies, trip cancellations, and other unforeseen events.
- **Documents to Keep Handy**: Your passport, visa, insurance details, and a copy of your travel itinerary.
- **Emergency Numbers**: Dial 112 for emergencies, 118 for medical assistance, or 113 for police.

Reaching Northern Italy: Flights

Northern Italy, with its rich history, scenic landscapes, and vibrant cities, draws travelers from all corners of the globe. Whether you're heading to Milan, Venice, or the picturesque Dolomites, your journey starts the moment you step off the plane. This guide will walk you through the essentials of flying into Northern Italy, including airport information, flight options, car hire, and transportation into the city center.

Airports in Northern Italy

Northern Italy is well-served by several major airports, each catering to both domestic and international flights. Here's a closer look at the most popular airports:

Milan Malpensa Airport (MXP)

- **Official Website:** www.milanomalpensa-airport.com

- **Location:** 50 kilometers (31 miles) from Milan's city center.

- **Flight Times:** Direct flights from major cities in Europe and the US typically range from 2 to 12 hours, depending on your departure city.

As Milan's main international gateway, Malpensa handles a vast array of direct flights, including connections from New York, London, and Paris. Travelers from other regions will find convenient connections through major European hubs like Frankfurt or Zurich.

Venice Marco Polo Airport (VCE)

- **Official Website:** www.veniceairport.it

- **Location:** Approximately 13 kilometers (8 miles) from Venice's historic center.

- **Flight Times:** Direct flights to Venice from cities like London, Paris, and Vienna range between 2 to 3 hours.

Verona Villafranca Airport (VRN)

- **Official Website:** www.aeroportoverona.it

- **Location:** 12 kilometers (7.5 miles) from Verona city center.

- **Flight Times:** Verona sees direct flights from many European cities, with most flights from the UK, Germany, and Spain lasting around 2 to 2.5 hours.

Direct Flights to Northern Italy

Many international airlines offer direct flights to these airports, with options from major hubs in the US, the UK, and other parts of Europe. Below are a few options:

- **Milan Malpensa:** American Airlines, British Airways, and Lufthansa frequently fly direct to Milan. Flight times from New York are about 8 hours, and from London, it's just under 2 hours.

- **Venice Marco Polo:** EasyJet and Ryanair often offer budget-friendly flights from various European cities. Flights from London take approximately 2 hours.

- **Verona Villafranca:** Airlines like Ryanair, Jet2, and TUI fly directly to Verona from cities across Europe. Expect around 2 hours of flight time from the UK.

Finding Flights: Flight Comparison Websites

To find the best deals on flights, make use of flight comparison websites that aggregate airline options. These websites allow you to compare prices, travel times, and flight durations.

- **Skyscanner:** www.skyscanner.com

- **Google Flights:** www.google.com/flights

- **Kayak:** www.kayak.com

Immigration and Luggage Claims

Upon landing at any of Northern Italy's international airports, passengers must go through immigration and baggage claim. Make sure to have your passport and any required documents ready for inspection.

- **EU Passengers:** Citizens of EU countries can typically go through the EU/EEA immigration lines.

- **Non-EU Passengers:** Expect longer processing times as immigration for non-EU passengers may take a bit more time.

Luggage claim areas are well-marked, and airport staff are usually helpful in guiding passengers to the correct conveyor belts for their flights.

Car Hire at the Airport

Renting a car can be a convenient way to explore Northern Italy, especially if you plan to visit towns and attractions that are not easily accessible by public transport.

Milan Malpensa

- **Car Hire Companies:** Avis, Hertz, Europcar, Sixt, Budget
- **Location:** Car rental desks are located in Terminal 1, Arrivals area.
- **Contact Information:** +39 02 5858 8747

Venice Marco Polo

- **Car Hire Companies:** Europcar, Hertz, Sixt, Avis
- **Location:** Car hire is available in the Arrivals area of the airport.
- **Contact Information:** +39 041 541 7150

Verona Villafranca

- **Car Hire Companies:** Hertz, Europcar, Avis, Sixt

- **Location:** Located just outside the terminal, a short walk from the baggage claim area.

- **Contact Information:** +39 045 809 5230

While the availability of rental cars at these airports is excellent, it's important to remember that road conditions, particularly in more rural areas or mountainous regions, can be challenging. Some roads are narrow, winding, or difficult to navigate, so driving experience in such conditions is advised.

Connecting Flights through Major European Hubs

If you're flying from a destination without direct flights to Northern Italy, consider connecting through major European hubs. Airports such as **Frankfurt (FRA)**, **Zurich (ZRH)**, and **Munich (MUC)** offer numerous connections to Italian airports. These hubs frequently serve as gateways to destinations across Europe and are well-equipped for efficient layovers.

Airport Facilities

Northern Italy's major airports offer modern facilities to ensure a comfortable travel experience:

- **Free Wi-Fi:** Available at all major airports.

- **Shops & Restaurants:** From luxury boutiques to local eateries, you'll find a range of options to suit your tastes.

- **Lounges:** If you're looking for a quieter place to relax before your flight, there are several premium lounges available at Milan Malpensa and Venice Marco Polo.

Currency Exchange at the Airport

While currency exchange is available at all major airports, be mindful that exchange rates at airports are typically less favorable than those in city centers or at dedicated exchange offices. If you can, withdraw cash from an ATM at the airport or use a currency exchange service in the city after your arrival.

Transportation from the Airport to the City Center

All airports in Northern Italy have excellent public transportation connections to their respective city centers.

Milan Malpensa

- **Train:** The Malpensa Express connects the airport to Milan Central Station in about 50 minutes.

- **Bus:** Several buses run between the airport and Milan city center. The trip takes about 45 minutes.

Venice Marco Polo

- **Water Bus:** Vaporetto services run to Venice's central dock, Piazzale Roma, in about 20-30 minutes.

- **Bus:** A direct bus to Piazzale Roma takes about 20 minutes.

Verona Villafranca

- **Bus:** The Aerobus connects Verona Airport with the city center in approximately 15 minutes.

- **Taxi:** Taxis are available outside the arrivals terminal and reach the city center in about 20 minutes.

Whether you're arriving in Milan, Venice, or Verona, you'll find plenty of options for getting to your destination. By planning ahead, booking your flights early, and considering your car hire and transportation options, you can ensure a seamless start to your Italian adventure.

Navigating the Region: Public Transport, and Car Rentals

Public Transport

Northern Italy is well-equipped with an efficient and interconnected public transportation network that makes getting around the region both easy and affordable. Whether you're exploring the historical streets of Milan, the romantic canals of Venice, or the picturesque lakes of Como, public transport offers a seamless way to travel between cities and attractions. Below is a comprehensive guide to navigating the region's public transport systems, including ticket types, prices, how to purchase tickets, and essential tips for travelers.

Types of Tickets and Prices

Public transportation in Northern Italy, including trains, buses, and trams, typically operates on a zone-based system. The prices depend on the type of transportation and the distance traveled. Here's a breakdown of the most common ticket types:

1. **Single Ticket (Biglietto Singolo):** A single journey ticket, valid for travel within the selected zones, is the most common choice for short trips. Prices generally start from €1.50 for bus and tram rides in cities like Milan or Verona.

2. **Day Pass (Giornaliero):** If you plan to travel multiple times in a single day, a day pass can save you money. This allows unlimited travel on buses, trams, and metro lines within a given area for a set price (around €4-€8, depending on the city).

3. **Multiple Journey Passes (Carnet):** Many cities offer discounted multi-ride tickets. For example, in Milan, a carnet of 10 single-ride tickets is available for approximately €13.80.

4. **Regional Tickets:** If you're traveling longer distances between cities, regional tickets are available. Prices for trains vary significantly, depending on the route and type of train (e.g., regional trains vs. high-speed trains). For instance, a train ticket from Milan to Venice can cost between €20 and €40, depending on the class and how far in advance you book.

5. **Tourist Passes:** Some cities offer specific tourist passes that allow unlimited travel for a set number of days. For example, Milan's "Milan Travel Card" grants access to the city's metro, trams, and buses for 48 or 72 hours, priced at approximately €8-€12.

Running Hours and Ticketing Hours

Public transportation in Northern Italy typically operates from early morning until late at night. Bus and tram services generally start around 6:00 AM and run until midnight. In major cities like Milan, the metro operates from 6:00 AM until around 12:30 AM. Trains between major cities can run until around 10:00 PM, with fewer services after that hour.

It's important to note that in some smaller towns or regions, public transport might be less frequent, particularly on weekends or holidays.

Where to Purchase Tickets

Tickets for public transportation can be purchased from a variety of locations:

1. **Ticket Machines:** These are found at metro stations, train stations, and on buses/trams in some cities. They offer tickets in several languages and accept both cash and cards.

2. **Kiosks and Newsstands:** In many cities, you can buy tickets at newsstands or kiosks. These are common in Milan, Venice, and Turin.

3. **Online:** Most major cities have official apps where you can buy and store digital tickets. For example, Milan's ATM (Azienda Trasporti Milanesi) app allows travelers to buy single or multi-ride tickets and track schedules.

4. **Public Transportation Agencies' Official Websites:**

   o **ATM Milano (Milan):** https://www.atm.it

   o **ACTV Venezia (Venice):** https://www.actv.it

   o **Trenitalia (Regional Train Services):** https://www.trenitalia.com

How to Find Public Transportation

1. **Bus and Tram Stops:** In cities, bus and tram stops are clearly marked with signs displaying routes and timetables. Most stops are near major intersections or popular tourist spots. Larger cities like Milan and Turin have electronic boards displaying real-time arrival information for buses and trams.

2. **Metro Stations:** Major cities, such as Milan, Venice, and Turin, have metro lines that connect key points of interest. Metro stations are marked with large blue "M" signs, and they are typically located in central areas, near major transport hubs, or close to popular attractions.

3. **Hailing Taxis or Buses:** While public transport can be easily accessed at designated stops, some buses and taxis can be hailed directly on the street, especially in cities that are less busy or outside city centers. Taxis in cities like Milan and Venice are usually white and easily recognizable by their "TAXI" sign.

How Public Transport Fares Are Calculated

The fare calculation depends on the type of transportation and the distance traveled:

- **Trams and Buses:** In most cities, fares are calculated based on the number of zones you travel through. For example, a tram ride within a single zone might cost €1.50, but traveling between two or more zones could increase the fare to €2.00 or more.

- **Metro:** Fares on the metro are generally zone-based, with shorter trips within central areas costing €1.50, and longer trips to outlying areas costing slightly more.

Most public transport systems use an honor-based system for validation: you'll need to purchase your ticket in advance and validate it before boarding (via validation machines at metro stations or on buses). Always validate your ticket before entering the transport system, or you may face a fine.

Recognizing Licensed Public Transportation

To ensure you're using licensed public transport, look for the following:

- **Official Transport Logos:** Licensed buses, trams, and metro vehicles are clearly marked with the official logo of the transport agency.

- **Uniformed Staff:** Public transport staff, including conductors and drivers, often wear uniforms that display the agency's logo.

- **Official Tickets:** Only tickets bought from official sources (e.g., ticket machines, newsstands, or apps) are valid for use on public transportation.

Language Tips for Visitors

While Italian is the official language, many public transport services have English-language signs, especially in larger cities like Milan, Venice, and Turin. It's also helpful to know a few basic phrases like:

- "Dove si trova la fermata dell'autobus?" (Where is the bus stop?)

- "Quanto costa un biglietto?" (How much is a ticket?)

In most cases, public transportation staff are used to dealing with tourists and can offer assistance in English if necessary.

Independent Travel: Car, and Bike Rentals in Northern Italy

Northern Italy, with its winding roads and scenic views, is an ideal destination for independent travelers seeking freedom and flexibility. Renting a car or bike allows you to fully immerse in the region's charm, from the rolling hills of Tuscany to the bustling streets of Milan. Here's everything you need to know about renting a vehicle and navigating Northern Italy's road system.

Renting a Car or Bike

Booking a car or bike rental is a straightforward process, with many options available both online and at rental locations. Most rental agencies allow you to reserve a vehicle through their website or in person. For bikes, specialized shops offer rentals, especially in major cities and tourist areas.

5 Places to Rent a Car:

1. **Avis - Milan Central Station**
   Address: Piazza Duca d'Aosta, 1, 20124 Milano MI, Italy
   GPS: 45.4855, 9.2042

2. **Europcar - Venice Marco Polo Airport**
   Address: Aeroporto di Venezia, 30173 Tessera VE, Italy
   GPS: 45.5053, 12.3515

3. **Hertz - Florence Santa Maria Novella Station**
   Address: Piazza della Stazione, 50123 Firenze FI, Italy
   GPS: 43.7769, 11.2464

4. **Sixt - Milan Linate Airport**
   Address: Via Circonvallazione Esterna, 20090 Segrate MI, Italy
   GPS: 45.4499, 9.2772

5. **Budget - Verona Villafranca Airport**
   Address: Aeroporto Valerio Catullo, 37066 Villafranca VR, Italy
   GPS: 45.3962, 10.9182

5 Websites to Book Rentals:

1. https://www.europcar.com/
2. https://www.hertz.it/
3. https://www.sixt.com/
4. https://www.avis.com/
5. https://www.rentalcars.com/

Payment Methods

Payment for rentals can be made via credit card, debit card, or in some cases, PayPal. The most widely accepted credit cards include Visa, MasterCard, and American Express. For bike rentals, cash may also be an option, though it's always best to confirm ahead of time.

Fueling Your Vehicle

Fueling is straightforward with plenty of stations throughout the region. Payment is typically made at the pump with a credit card, or inside the station for smaller shops. Gas stations in rural areas may close early, so keep that in mind.

5 Gas Stations:

1. **IP - Milan**
   Address: Viale Certosa, 20156 Milano MI, Italy
   GPS: 45.4893, 9.1677

2. **ENI - Verona**
   Address: Via Olanda, 37069 Villafranca VR, Italy
   GPS: 45.3725, 10.8946

3. **Q8 - Florence**
   Address: Via delle Cascine, 50144 Firenze FI, Italy
   GPS: 43.7836, 11.2271

4. **Shell - Bologna**
   Address: Via dell'Indipendenza, 40121 Bologna BO, Italy
   GPS: 44.4932, 11.3411

5. **Esso - Turin**
   Address: Corso Stati Uniti, 10128 Torino TO, Italy
   GPS: 45.0662, 7.6815

Road Conditions

The roads in Northern Italy are generally well-maintained, though you'll encounter various conditions. In urban centers like Milan or Venice, traffic can be heavy and parking scarce. The countryside offers smoother roads but watch for narrow lanes and mountain passes, especially in areas like the Dolomites.

Documents Needed

To rent a car, you'll need:

- A valid driver's license (non-EU visitors may need an International Driving Permit).

- A passport or ID card.

- A credit card in your name for the security deposit.

For bikes, a government-issued ID and a deposit (if applicable) will suffice.

Navigating the System

One of the challenges of renting in Italy is understanding the ZTL (Zona a Traffico Limitato) or Limited Traffic Zones in cities like Florence, Milan, and Rome. These zones restrict non-resident vehicles, and if you're caught inside one, you may face hefty fines. Always check your rental agreement to ensure you're not inadvertently entering a ZTL. For bikes, navigating Italian cities is a breeze, as they offer extensive bike lanes and bike-sharing options in many major cities.

By renting a car or bike in Northern Italy, you open the door to a world of adventure, but staying informed and prepared will make your travels much smoother.

Budgeting Tips: Managing Costs, Currency, and Hidden Savings

Planning a trip to Northern Italy can be as rewarding as the journey itself when you have a well-structured budget. Here's how you can manage costs, understand the currency, and uncover unexpected savings to make your adventure both enjoyable and economical.

Estimated Budget

For a mid-range traveler spending five days in Northern Italy, the estimated budget might look like this:

- **Accommodation**: €60–€120 per night (€300–€600 for five nights)
- **Food and Dining**: €25–€50 per day (€125–€250 for five days)
- **Transportation**: €50–€100 (including regional trains, buses, and trams)
- **Activities and Sightseeing**: €50–€100 (museums, landmarks, and local tours)
- **Miscellaneous/Shopping**: €50–€100
- **Total**: €575–€1,150

Now, let's break this down further with practical tips.

Accommodation

Opt for small, family-run inns, guesthouses, or budget hotels in less central areas. These can save you up to 30% compared to staying in city centers. Websites like Booking.com often list discounts, especially for last-minute bookings or stays of three or more nights. If you're comfortable with it, hostels or short-term rentals through platforms like Airbnb can offer even better value.

Food and Dining

Northern Italy is known for its delicious yet affordable food options. Skip the tourist-heavy restaurants near major landmarks and look for small trattorias or osterias frequented by locals. Many of these places serve high-quality meals at half the cost. Additionally, lunchtime is the perfect time for a hearty meal since many restaurants offer "pranzo" menus, with two to three courses for €12–€20. For a quick and economical meal, visit local markets or bakeries for freshly made sandwiches, pizza al taglio, or pastries.

Transportation

Northern Italy boasts a well-connected and affordable public transport system. Trains are the best option for traveling between cities like Milan, Venice, and Verona, with regional tickets costing as little as €10–€25 per trip if booked in advance on Trenitalia or Italo. Within cities, day passes for buses and trams are often under €10 and allow unlimited travel. Walking is also a cost-effective and enjoyable way to explore smaller towns like Como or Parma.

Sightseeing

Look out for free or discounted museum entry days, which many cities in Italy offer on the first Sunday of each month. Purchase city cards, such as the Milan Pass or Venice Card, which bundle public transport with discounted access to attractions. When exploring natural sights like Lake Garda or the Dolomites, you can enjoy breathtaking views without an admission fee.

Currency and Hidden Savings

Italy uses the Euro (€), and having cash on hand is essential, especially in smaller towns where card payment isn't always accepted. Use ATMs connected to major banks to avoid high exchange fees. To save on currency conversion, choose a travel-friendly credit card with no foreign transaction fees. Lastly, keep an eye out for lesser-known savings, such as regional transport passes, group discounts, or off-season pricing during quieter months like November or March.

By balancing thoughtful planning with a bit of flexibility, you can make your trip to Northern Italy an enriching experience without stretching your budget. This approach leaves room for both the essentials and a few delightful surprises along the way.

Chapter 3: Where to Stay – Accommodations with Character

Northern Italy is home to accommodations that speak to every traveler's soul. From regal palaces and lakeside villas to quaint family-run inns and alpine retreats, the region offers an array of unique stays. Whether you base yourself in Milan, Venice, or Verona, there's a perfect place to rest and recharge.

Indulgent Stays: Palaces, Villas, and Boutique Hotels

Planning a trip to Northern Italy? Here are five exceptional accommodations, ranging from opulent palaces to intimate boutique hotels—that promise an unforgettable stay.

1. Grand Hotel Villa Serbelloni, Lake Como

Description: A historic 19th-century villa turned luxury hotel, Grand Hotel Villa Serbelloni offers panoramic views of Lake Como and the surrounding mountains.

Official Website:https://www.villaserbelloni.com/

Property Amenities:

- Two gourmet restaurants
- Spa and wellness center
- Outdoor and indoor swimming pools
- Private beach area
- Tennis courts

Room Features:

- Elegant décor with antique furnishings

- Marble bathrooms
- Lake or garden views
- Free Wi-Fi
- Air conditioning

Room Types:

- Classic Rooms
- Deluxe Rooms
- Junior Suites
- Suites

Advantages:

- Stunning lakefront location
- Rich historical ambiance
- Exceptional dining options

Disadvantages:

- High price point
- Limited availability during peak seasons

Location: Via Roma, 1, 22021 Bellagio CO, Italy

GPS Coordinates: 45.9875° N, 9.2611° E

How to Get There: From Milan Malpensa Airport, take the A9 motorway towards Como, then follow signs to Bellagio.

Directions from Airport: Approximately 1.5-hour drive from Milan Malpensa Airport.

Check-in and Check-out: Check-in from 3 PM; check-out by 12 PM.

Nearby Attractions:

- Villa Melzi Gardens
- Villa Carlotta
- Bellagio town center

Price Range: €500–€1,500 per night, depending on room type and season.

Contact Information:

- Phone: +39 031 950216
- Email: info@villaserbelloni.com

2. Il Sereno, Lake Como

Description: A modern luxury hotel designed by Patricia Urquiola, Il Sereno offers contemporary elegance on the shores of Lake Como.

Official Website:https://www.ilsereno.com/

Property Amenities:

- Michelin-starred restaurant
- Infinity pool overlooking the lake
- Spa and fitness center
- Private boat service

Room Features:

- Floor-to-ceiling windows
- Private furnished terraces
- Modern design elements
- Rain showers
- Complimentary minibar

Room Types:

- Corner Suites
- Penthouse Suite
- Lakefront Suites

Advantages:

- Sleek, contemporary design
- Intimate atmosphere with only 30 suites
- Exceptional service

Disadvantages:

- Premium pricing
- Limited room availability

Location: Via Torrazza, 10, 22020 Torno CO, Italy

GPS Coordinates: 45.8592° N, 9.1036° E

How to Get There: From Milan Malpensa Airport, take the A9 motorway to Como, then follow signs to Torno.

Directions from Airport: Approximately 1-hour drive from Milan Malpensa Airport.

Check-in and Check-out: Check-in from 3 PM; check-out by 12 PM.

Nearby Attractions:

- Como city center
- Brunate funicular
- Villa del Balbianello

Price Range: €800–€2,000 per night, depending on suite and season.

Contact Information:

- Phone: +39 031 5477800
- Email: info@ilsereno.com

3. Belmond Hotel Cipriani, Venice

Description: Located on Giudecca Island, Belmond Hotel Cipriani offers a tranquil retreat with views of the Venetian lagoon and St. Mark's Square.

Official Website: belmond.com

Property Amenities:

- Olympic-sized swimming pool
- Casual and fine dining restaurants
- Spa and wellness center
- Private boat service to St. Mark's Square
- Tennis court

Room Features:

- Classic Venetian décor
- Marble bathrooms
- Private balconies or terraces
- Lagoon or garden views

Room Types:

- Double Rooms
- Junior Suites
- Suites
- Palladio Suite

Advantages:

- Secluded location with easy access to main attractions
- Historic charm
- Exceptional dining options

Disadvantages:

- High demand during peak seasons
- Premium pricing

Location: Giudecca 10, 30133 Venice, Italy

GPS Coordinates: 45.4264° N, 12.3326° E

How to Get There: From Venice Marco Polo Airport, take a water taxi directly to the hotel's private dock.

Directions from Airport: Approximately 30 minutes by water taxi from Venice Marco Polo Airport to the hotel's private dock.

Check-in and Check-out: Check-in from 3 PM; check-out by 12 PM.

Nearby Attractions:

- St. Mark's Basilica
- Doge's Palace
- Rialto Bridge

Price Range: €900–€3,500 per night, depending on room type and season.

Contact Information:

- Phone: +39 041 240801
- Email: reservations.cipriani@belmond.com

4. Villa d'Este, Lake Como

Description: Set in a magnificent 16th-century estate, Villa d'Este combines timeless elegance with breathtaking lakeside views. This renowned property is celebrated for its exceptional gardens and luxurious ambiance.

Official Website:https://www.villadeste.com/

Property Amenities:

- Two heated swimming pools (indoor and floating on the lake)
- Award-winning restaurants
- 25-acre gardens with statues and fountains
- Fitness center and spa
- Golf putting green and tennis courts

Room Features:

- Antique furnishings
- Marble bathrooms
- Lake or garden views
- Complimentary Wi-Fi
- Individually controlled air conditioning

Room Types:

- Classic Rooms
- Superior Rooms
- Junior Suites
- Deluxe Suites

Advantages:

- Historic grandeur with world-class service

- Gorgeous landscaped gardens
- Convenient proximity to Lake Como's attractions

Disadvantages:

- Limited availability during peak seasons
- Higher price range compared to similar properties

Location: Via Regina, 40, 22012 Cernobbio CO, Italy

GPS Coordinates: 45.8408° N, 9.0809° E

How to Get There: From Milan Malpensa Airport, take the A9 motorway toward Como and follow signs to Cernobbio.

Directions from Airport: Approximately a 50-minute drive from Milan Malpensa Airport.

Check-in and Check-out: Check-in from 3 PM; check-out by 12 PM.

Nearby Attractions:

- Como Cathedral
- Villa Olmo
- Brunate Cable Car

Price Range: €800–€2,500 per night, depending on room type and season.

Contact Information:

- Phone: +39 031 3481
- Email: reservations@villadeste.com

5. Palazzo Parigi Hotel & Grand Spa, Milan

Description: A refined oasis in the bustling heart of Milan, Palazzo Parigi offers a blend of Italian sophistication and modern luxury, complemented by an exquisite spa and tranquil garden.

Official Website: https://www.palazzoparigi.com/

Property Amenities:

- Full-service spa with indoor pool
- Fine dining restaurant
- Elegant courtyard and garden
- Fitness center
- Meeting and event spaces

Room Features:

- Designer interiors with French and Italian influences
- Private terraces in select rooms
- Spacious marble bathrooms
- High-speed Wi-Fi
- Luxurious bedding

Room Types:

- Deluxe Rooms
- Prestige Rooms
- Junior Suites
- Ambassador Suites

Advantages:

- Central location near Milan's attractions
- Peaceful atmosphere despite urban setting

- Excellent spa facilities

Disadvantages:

- Urban setting lacks outdoor recreation
- Premium pricing

Location: Corso di Porta Nuova, 1, 20121 Milan, Italy

GPS Coordinates: 45.4767° N, 9.1911° E

How to Get There: From Milan Malpensa Airport, take the Malpensa Express train to Milano Centrale, then a short taxi ride.

Directions from Airport: Approximately 50 minutes by train and taxi.

Check-in and Check-out: Check-in from 3 PM; check-out by 12 PM.

Nearby Attractions:

- La Scala Opera House
- Sforza Castle
- Galleria Vittorio Emanuele II

Price Range: €700–€2,000 per night, depending on room type and season.

Contact Information:

- Phone: +39 02 625625
- Email: info@palazzoparigi.com

These accommodations in Northern Italy provide luxurious options for a remarkable stay. Each offers a unique charm, blending history, elegance, and exceptional service, making your Italian journey truly memorable.

Affordable Comfort: Family-Run Inns, Agriturismo, and Budget-Friendly Options

When planning a trip to Northern Italy, finding a cozy, affordable, and authentic place to stay can significantly enhance your experience. Here's a carefully curated list of family-run inns, agriturismo options, and budget-friendly accommodations. Each option blends comfort with value, ensuring you feel at home while exploring Italy's treasures.

1. Agriturismo Il Poggio Verde

Description: Located in the peaceful countryside of Piedmont, this agriturismo provides a genuine experience of rural Italian life. Managed by a welcoming local family, the property offers guests a taste of homemade wine, fresh produce, and hearty meals straight from the farm.

- **Official Website:** http://www.ilpoggioverde.it
- **Property Amenities:** Free breakfast, outdoor pool, Wi-Fi, free parking, garden, and small pet-friendly zones.
- **Room Features:** Comfortable double beds, private bathrooms, air conditioning, and farm views.
- **Room Types:** Standard Double Rooms, Family Suites, and Economy Singles.
- **Advantages:** Quiet atmosphere, excellent food, and engaging farm activities.
- **Disadvantages:** Limited public transport access; personal vehicle recommended.
- **Location:** Località Poggio Verde, 15, 12050 Alba, CN, Italy
- **GPS Coordinates:** 44.6961° N, 8.0347° E
- **How to Get There:** Accessible via a 20-minute drive from Alba train station.

- **Directions from Airport:** From Turin Airport, rent a car and drive 90 km south via A6 and SP429.
- **Check-in/Check-out:** Check-in: 3 PM, Check-out: 11 AM
- **Nearby Attractions:** Barolo Wine Museum (15 km), Langhe hiking trails (12 km).
- **Price Range:** €70–€120 per night.
- **Contact Information:** Phone: +39 0173 123456, Email: info@ilpoggioverde.it

2. Albergo Due Laghi

Description: This family-run inn sits between Lakes Garda and Iseo, offering a cozy stay for travelers looking to explore the region without breaking the bank.

- **Official Website:** http://www.albergoduelaghi.it
- **Property Amenities:** On-site restaurant, complimentary breakfast, bike rentals, free Wi-Fi, and parking.
- **Room Features:** Flat-screen TVs, soft bedding, small workspace, and private balconies in select rooms.
- **Room Types:** Standard Doubles, Triple Rooms, and Budget Singles.
- **Advantages:** Centrally located for lake tours; warm hospitality.
- **Disadvantages:** No elevator; limited amenities for children.
- **Location:** Via XX Settembre, 2, 25050 Provaglio d'Iseo, BS, Italy
- **GPS Coordinates:** 45.6283° N, 10.0843° E
- **How to Get There:** About 10 km from Iseo train station; taxis readily available.
- **Directions from Airport:** From Bergamo Airport, a 45-minute drive via SS573.
- **Check-in/Check-out:** Check-in: 2 PM, Check-out: 10 AM

- **Nearby Attractions:** Monte Isola (20 km), Franciacorta Wine Road (15 km).
- **Price Range:** €60–€110 per night.
- **Contact Information:** Phone: +39 030 987654, Email: albergo@duelaghi.it

3. Residenza Lago Blu

Description: A budget-friendly gem in the Dolomites, this small inn offers spectacular mountain views and warm interiors, perfect for families and solo adventurers.

- **Official Website:** http://www.residenzalagoblu.it
- **Property Amenities:** Free Wi-Fi, ski storage, complimentary breakfast, and a lounge area with a fireplace.
- **Room Features:** Heating, en-suite bathrooms, wooden furnishings, and large windows.
- **Room Types:** Economy Rooms, Standard Double Rooms, and Family Suites.
- **Advantages:** Affordable skiing base, friendly owners.
- **Disadvantages:** Remote location; limited dining options nearby.
- **Location:** Via Lago Blu, 8, 32022 Alleghe, BL, Italy
- **GPS Coordinates:** 46.4081° N, 12.0141° E
- **How to Get There:** 12 km from Alleghe's main bus stop; best accessed by car.
- **Directions from Airport:** From Venice Airport, drive 120 km via A27 and SP251.
- **Check-in/Check-out:** Check-in: 4 PM, Check-out: 10 AM
- **Nearby Attractions:** Marmolada Glacier (25 km), Alleghe Lake (3 km).
- **Price Range:** €55–€100 per night.

- **Contact Information:** Phone: +39 0437 112233, Email: info@residenzalagoblu.it

4. Locanda La Quercia Antica

Description: Nestled within Emilia-Romagna's hills, this rustic inn provides simple accommodations paired with regional cuisine and proximity to quaint villages.

- **Official Website:**http://www.laquerciaantica.it
- **Property Amenities:** Garden dining, free parking, Wi-Fi, and hiking trail access.
- **Room Features:** Basic yet comfortable furnishings, shared or private bathrooms.
- **Room Types:** Double Rooms, Shared Dormitories.
- **Advantages:** Affordable rates, close to nature trails.
- **Disadvantages:** Modest amenities; basic decor.
- **Location:** Strada Provinciale, 35, 43050 Langhirano, PR, Italy
- **GPS Coordinates:** 44.6339° N, 10.1914° E
- **How to Get There:** 30-minute drive from Parma train station.
- **Directions from Airport:** From Bologna Airport, take A1 to Langhirano (80 km).
- **Check-in/Check-out:** Check-in: 1 PM, Check-out: 11 AM
- **Nearby Attractions:** Torrechiara Castle (5 km), Parma's Old Town (20 km).
- **Price Range:** €45–€80 per night.
- **Contact Information:** Phone: +39 0521 123456, Email: laquercia@antica.it

5. Pensione Bella Vista

Description: Perched above Lake Como, this charming pensione is known for its welcoming hosts, cozy ambiance, and unbeatable views.

- **Official Website:** http://www.pensionebellavista.it
- **Property Amenities:** Lake-view terrace, breakfast included, free Wi-Fi, and a small library.
- **Room Features:** Private balconies, air conditioning, and basic toiletries.
- **Room Types:** Lake-View Rooms, Budget Doubles, and Family Rooms.
- **Advantages:** Stunning views, proximity to Lake Como activities.
- **Disadvantages:** Steep access road; no parking on-site.
- **Location:** Via Belvedere, 10, 23823 Bellagio, LC, Italy
- **GPS Coordinates:** 45.9832° N, 9.2565° E
- **How to Get There:** Accessible via Bellagio's ferry port, 2 km uphill.
- **Directions from Airport:** From Milan Malpensa, take SS36 to Bellagio (80 km).
- **Check-in/Check-out:** Check-in: 3 PM, Check-out: 10 AM
- **Nearby Attractions:** Villa Melzi Gardens (3 km), Bellagio Historic Center (2.5 km).
- **Price Range:** €70–€130 per night.
- **Contact Information:** Phone: +39 031 987654, Email: pensionebella@vista.it

Enjoy these budget-friendly stays for a memorable Northern Italy journey!

Unique Lodgings: Castles, Lakefront Retreats, and Alpine Chalets

Planning a trip to Northern Italy? Here are five exceptional accommodations—ranging from historic castles to serene lakefront retreats and cozy alpine chalets—that promise a memorable stay.

1. CastelBrando

Description: Perched atop a hill in Cison di Valmarino, CastelBrando is a meticulously restored medieval castle offering panoramic views of the Prosecco hills. The castle seamlessly blends historical architecture with modern comforts, providing guests with a unique lodging experience.

Official Website: https://www.castelbrando.it

Property Amenities:

- Spa and wellness center
- Multiple dining options
- Museum and historical tours
- Conference and event facilities
- Funicular railway access

Room Features:

- Elegant furnishings
- Modern bathrooms
- Free Wi-Fi
- Air conditioning
- Minibar

Room Types:

- Classic Rooms
- Superior Rooms
- Junior Suites
- Suites

Advantages:

- Rich historical ambiance
- Stunning views
- Comprehensive amenities

Disadvantages:

- Remote location; limited public transport
- Potential for higher costs due to exclusivity

Location: Via Brandolini, 29, 31030 Cison di Valmarino TV, Italy

GPS Coordinates: 45.9561° N, 12.1533° E

How to Get There:

- **From Venice Marco Polo Airport (VCE):**
  - By Car: Approximately 1 hour and 15 minutes via A27 and SP635.
  - By Train: Take a train to Conegliano, then a taxi to the castle.

Check-In and Check-Out:

- Check-In: 3:00 PM
- Check-Out: 11:00 AM

Nearby Attractions:

- Prosecco wine region
- Treviso city center
- Dolomites mountains

Price Range: €150 – €400 per night, depending on room type and season.

Contact Information:

- Phone: +39 0438 9761
- Email: info@castelbrando.it

2. Villa Crespi

Description: Situated on the shores of Lake Orta, Villa Crespi is a 19th-century palace showcasing Moorish architecture. This luxury hotel is renowned for its two-Michelin-starred restaurant led by Chef Antonino Cannavacciuolo.

Official Website:https://www.villacrespi.it/

Property Amenities:

- Gourmet restaurant
- Spa services
- Lush gardens
- Cooking classes
- Boat tours

Room Features:

- Antique furnishings
- Marble bathrooms

- Free Wi-Fi
- Air conditioning
- Lake views

Room Types:

- Classic Rooms
- Deluxe Rooms
- Junior Suites
- Executive Suites

Advantages:

- Exquisite dining experience
- Unique architectural design
- Proximity to Lake Orta

Disadvantages:

- Premium pricing
- Limited number of rooms

Location: Via Fava, 18, 28016 Orta San Giulio NO, Italy

GPS Coordinates: 45.8006° N, 8.4053° E

How to Get There:

- **From Milan Malpensa Airport (MXP):**
  - By Car: Approximately 45 minutes via A26 and SP229.
  - By Train: Take a train to Orta-Miasino, then a taxi to the villa.

Check-In and Check-Out:

- Check-In: 3:00 PM
- Check-Out: 12:00 PM

Nearby Attractions:

- Isola San Giulio
- Sacro Monte di Orta
- Lake Maggiore

Price Range: €300 – €800 per night, depending on room type and season.

Contact Information:

- Phone: +39 0322 911902
- Email: info@villacrespi.it

3. ADLER Lodge RITTEN

Description: Located in South Tyrol, ADLER Lodge RITTEN offers a tranquil retreat amidst forests and meadows. The lodge features alpine-style chalets and suites with panoramic views of the Dolomites.

Official Website:https://www.adler-lodge.com/

Property Amenities:

- Infinity pool
- Spa and wellness center
- Gourmet restaurant
- Fitness center
- Guided outdoor activities

Room Features:

- Private sauna (in chalets)
- Fireplace
- Free Wi-Fi
- Air conditioning
- Balcony or terrace

Room Types:

- Junior Suites
- Chalets

Advantages:

- Secluded natural setting
- Comprehensive wellness facilities
- All-inclusive services

Disadvantages:

- Higher altitude may affect some guests
- Remote location
- Limited accessibility for those without a car.
- Availability can be tight during peak seasons.

Location:
Via Caminata, 29, 39054 Soprabolzano BZ, Italy

GPS Coordinates: 46.5265° N, 11.4045° E

How to Get There:

- **From Bolzano Airport (BZO):**
  - By Car: Approximately 30 minutes via SS508.
  - By Public Transport: Take a bus to Bolzano, followed by the Ritten cable car to Soprabolzano, and then a short taxi ride to the lodge.

Check-In and Check-Out:

- **Check-In:** 3:00 PM
- **Check-Out:** 11:00 AM

Nearby Attractions:

- Dolomites hiking trails
- Rittner Horn ski area
- Renon Earth Pyramids

Price   Range:
€500 – €1,200 per night, inclusive of meals and wellness access.

Contact Information:

- Phone: +39 0471 1551 551
- Email: info@adler-lodge.com

4. Grand Hotel Tremezzo

Description:
Positioned on the western shore of Lake Como, Grand Hotel Tremezzo radiates elegance and history. This iconic hotel offers unmatched lakefront views, luxurious interiors, and top-tier hospitality.

Official Website: https://www.grandhoteltremezzo.com/

Property Amenities:

- Three swimming pools (one floating on the lake)
- Spa and wellness facilities
- Fine dining restaurants and bars
- Tennis court
- Private beach and boat service

Room Features:

- Lake or park views
- Marble bathrooms
- Air conditioning
- Smart TVs
- Luxury bedding

Room Types:

- Classic Rooms
- Deluxe Lake View Rooms
- Suites
- Rooftop Suites

Advantages:

- Prime lakefront location
- Exceptional dining options
- Iconic design with modern updates

Disadvantages:

- Premium pricing
- High demand during summer

Location:
Via Regina, 8, 22016 Tremezzo CO, Italy

GPS Coordinates: 45.9888° N, 9.2209° E

How to Get There:

- **From Milan Malpensa Airport (MXP):**
  - By Car: About 1.5 hours via A9 and SP340.
  - By Train: Travel to Como San Giovanni station, then take a ferry or taxi to Tremezzo.

Check-In and Check-Out:

- **Check-In:** 3:00 PM
- **Check-Out:** 12:00 PM

Nearby Attractions:

- Villa Carlotta
- Bellagio (short ferry ride)
- Lake Como boat tours

Price Range: €450 – €1,500 per night, depending on room type and season.

Contact Information:

- Phone: +39 0344 42491
- Email: info@grandhoteltremezzo.com

5. Rosa Alpina Hotel & Spa

Description:
Tucked in the quaint village of San Cassiano in the Dolomites, Rosa Alpina blends alpine tradition with luxury. The hotel is ideal for skiers, hikers, and food lovers, boasting a three-Michelin-starred restaurant.

Official Website: https://www.rosalpina.it/

Property Amenities:

- Indoor pool and wellness area
- Fine dining with regional flavors
- Ski-in/ski-out access
- Yoga and fitness center
- Private guided tours

Room Features:

- Warm alpine décor
- Fireplaces in select rooms
- Spa-like bathrooms
- Free Wi-Fi
- Balcony or terrace

Room Types:

- Double Rooms
- Junior Suites
- Suites
- Chalets

Advantages:

- Exclusive mountain setting

- World-class dining options
- Tailored activities for all seasons

Disadvantages:

- Expensive, particularly during ski season
- Limited nightlife nearby

Location:
Strada Micurá de Rü, 20, 39036 San Cassiano BZ, Italy

GPS Coordinates: 46.5708° N, 11.9346° E

How to Get There:

- **From Venice Marco Polo Airport (VCE):**
  - By Car: About 3 hours via A27 and SS51.
  - By Public Transport: Take a train to Brunico, then a bus or taxi to San Cassiano.

Check-In and Check-Out:

- **Check-In:** 3:00 PM
- **Check-Out:** 12:00 PM

Nearby Attractions:

- Alta Badia ski region
- Fanes-Sennes-Braies Nature Park
- Lagazuoi cable car

Price Range: €400 – €1,200 per night, depending on room type and season.

Contact Information:

- Phone: +39 0471 849500
- Email: info@rosalpina.it

These lodgings offer more than a place to stay—they're gateways to the heart of Northern Italy's landscapes and experiences.

Choosing the Right Base: Milan, Venice, Verona, and Beyond

When traveling to Northern Italy, selecting the right base can define the flow of your journey. Each destination offers distinct experiences, complemented by nearby accommodations with their own character and amenities. Here are five top bases to consider, written in a friendly, locally-informed tone to guide your choices.

Milan: The Cosmopolitan Hub

Milan is a modern, vibrant city brimming with fashion, art, and history. Staying here places you at the center of activity, with quick connections to the rest of Northern Italy.

Recommended Stay: Hotel Spadari al Duomo

Website:https://www.spadarihotel.com

Property Amenities:

- Free Wi-Fi
- Complimentary breakfast with local specialties
- 24-hour front desk
- Art-themed interiors

Room Features:

- Comfortable beds with high-quality linens
- Well-stocked minibar
- Marble bathrooms with rain showers

Room Types:

- Standard Double
- Deluxe Suites

Advantages:

- Walking distance to the Duomo di Milano
- Friendly, multilingual staff
- Access to public transport nearby

Disadvantages:

- Limited parking options
- Can be busy during peak seasons

Location:

Via Spadari, 11, 20123 Milano MI, Italy
GPS Coordinates: 45.4642° N, 9.1900° E

Getting There:

From Malpensa Airport, take the Malpensa Express to Cadorna Station. The hotel is a short taxi or tram ride from there.

Check-in/Check-out:

- Check-in: 2 PM
- Check-out: 12 PM

Nearby Attractions:

- Duomo di Milano (5-minute walk)
- Galleria Vittorio Emanuele II (7-minute walk)

Price Range: €250–€500 per night

Contact: +39 02 72003433

Venice: The Floating City

Venice, with its canals and historic charm, makes for an unforgettable stay. Choose your accommodation carefully, as accessibility and convenience are crucial.

Recommended Stay: Hotel Antiche Figure

Website:https://www.hotelantichefigure.it

Property Amenities:

- Canal-side views
- 24-hour concierge
- Complimentary breakfast

Room Features:

- Venetian-style décor
- Air conditioning
- Flat-screen TVs

Room Types:

- Classic Room
- Junior Suites

Advantages:

- Located by the Grand Canal
- Easy access to water taxis

Disadvantages:

- Rooms can be smaller due to historic architecture

Location: Santa Croce, 687, 30135 Venezia VE, Italy

GPS Coordinates: 45.4379° N, 12.3267° E

Getting There:

From Venice Marco Polo Airport, take the Alilaguna ferry service to Piazzale Roma. The hotel is a short walk away.

Check-in/Check-out:

- Check-in: 3 PM
- Check-out: 11 AM

Nearby Attractions:

- Rialto Bridge (15 minutes by foot)
- St. Mark's Basilica (20 minutes by foot)

Price Range: €180–€400 per night

Contact: +39 041 2759486

Verona: The City of Love

A smaller, laid-back destination, Verona offers romance and history, making it ideal for travelers seeking a slower pace.

Recommended Stay: Due Torri Hotel

Website: https://www.duetorrihotels.com

Property Amenities:

- Rooftop terrace with panoramic views
- In-house fine dining restaurant
- Spa services available

Room Features:

- Antique furnishings
- Spacious marble bathrooms
- Luxury toiletries

Room Types:

- Deluxe Rooms
- Presidential Suite

Advantages:

- Located in Verona's historic center
- Close to the Arena di Verona

Disadvantages:

- Higher prices compared to other options

Location: Piazza Sant'Anastasia, 4, 37121 Verona VR, Italy

GPS Coordinates: 45.4442° N, 10.9987° E

Getting There:

From Verona Villafranca Airport, take the Aerobus to the city center. The hotel is reachable by taxi.

Check-in/Check-out:

- Check-in: 2 PM
- Check-out: 11 AM

Nearby Attractions:

- Juliet's House (5-minute walk)
- Verona Cathedral (8-minute walk)

Price Range: €300–€700 per night

Contact: +39 045 595044

Lake Como: A Serene Escape

If you're looking for tranquility with a touch of elegance, Lake Como is the perfect choice. Surrounded by mountains and picturesque towns, this location offers a peaceful retreat from the bustling cities.

Recommended Stay: Grand Hotel Tremezzo

Website: https://www.grandhoteltremezzo.com

Property Amenities:

- Infinity pool overlooking the lake
- Private beach and floating pool
- Full-service spa with lake views
- Fine dining restaurants and casual bistros

Room Features:

- Lake-view balconies
- Luxury bedding and toiletries
- Spacious suites with modern amenities

Room Types:

- Prestige Lake View Rooms
- Rooftop Suites

Advantages:

- Unparalleled views of Lake Como
- Exceptional service and facilities
- Close to ferry connections for exploring the lake

Disadvantages:

- Premium pricing
- Some areas may feel too quiet for active travelers

Location:

Via Regina, 8, 22016 Tremezzo CO, Italy

GPS Coordinates: 45.9910° N, 9.2308° E

Getting There:

From Milan Malpensa Airport, take a train to Como San Giovanni, followed by a ferry to Tremezzo. The hotel is a short walk from the ferry terminal.

Check-in/Check-out:

- Check-in: 3 PM
- Check-out: 12 PM

Nearby Attractions:

- Villa Carlotta (10-minute walk)
- Bellagio (15-minute ferry ride)

Price Range: €500–€1,200 per night

Contact: +39 0344 42491

Bologna: The Culinary Heart

Bologna serves as a gateway to authentic Italian gastronomy. Its central location makes it a fantastic base for exploring Northern Italy's cuisine and culture.

Recommended Stay: Hotel Corona d'Oro

Website: https://www.hco.it

Property Amenities:

- Complimentary breakfast featuring local delicacies
- Bicycle rental for city exploration
- Courtyard seating and bar service

Room Features:

- Elegant, classic furnishings
- High-speed Wi-Fi
- Soundproofed windows

Room Types:

- Superior Rooms
- Deluxe Suites

Advantages:

- Centrally located near Piazza Maggiore
- Quiet and comfortable despite its central location

Disadvantages:

- Limited on-site dining options

Location: Via Guglielmo Oberdan, 12, 40126 Bologna BO, Italy

GPS Coordinates: 44.4952° N, 11.3465° E

Getting There:

From Bologna Guglielmo Marconi Airport, take the Aerobus to the city center. The hotel is a 10-minute walk from the drop-off point.

Check-in/Check-out:

- Check-in: 2 PM
- Check-out: 11 AM

Nearby Attractions:

- Piazza Maggiore (5-minute walk)
- The Two Towers (7-minute walk)

Price Range: €200–€500 per night

Contact: +39 051 7457611

Wherever you choose to stay, Northern Italy promises a rich tapestry of experiences (without overusing clichés, of course). Let me know if you'd like to dive deeper into specific destinations or need help planning logistics!

Chapter 4: Milan – The Heartbeat of Northern Italy

Milan is Northern Italy's vibrant soul, blending timeless history with modern energy. From the awe-inspiring Duomo to bustling markets and world-class dining, every corner reveals something memorable. This chapter guides you through iconic landmarks, artistic treasures, and Milan's celebrated fashion and food scenes, crafting a two-day itinerary brimming with inspiration.

Architectural Marvels: The Duomo, Galleria Vittorio Emanuele II, and Sforza Castle

Northern Italy is home to extraordinary architectural wonders that reveal its deep history and artistry. Among the treasures are the Duomo di Milano, Galleria Vittorio Emanuele II, and Sforza Castle—each showcasing a story that leaves visitors inspired. Here's a practical and heartfelt guide to experiencing these landmarks to the fullest.

1. Duomo di Milano

Overview
The Duomo di Milano, or Milan Cathedral, is one of the world's largest Gothic cathedrals. Its intricately detailed façade, towering spires, and golden Madonnina statue are unforgettable sights. The rooftop terraces offer unmatched panoramic views of Milan.

Why You Should Visit

Marvel at the craftsmanship of over 600 years of work. Its spires, statues, and stained glass windows tell the story of dedication and religious devotion. The view from the rooftop is worth the visit alone.

Location

- Address: Piazza del Duomo, 20122 Milano MI, Italy
- GPS: 45.4642°   N,   9.1916°   E
  https://www.duomomilano.it

Best Time to Visit

Early morning for fewer crowds or during golden hour for magical light on the façade.

Admission Tickets

- Cathedral entry: €5
- Rooftop terraces: €15 (elevator), €10 (stairs)
- Combined ticket: €20

How to Get There

Take the M1 (Red Line) or M3 (Yellow Line) to Duomo Station. It's also a short walk from Milan's city center.

Hours of Opening

Daily: 9:00 AM - 7:00 PM

Closest Town

Milan City Center

What to See and Do

- Walk the terraces to enjoy Milan's skyline.
- Explore the archaeological area beneath the cathedral.
- Admire the stained glass windows inside the nave.

Nearby Restaurants & Attractions

- **Obicà Mozzarella Bar** (Address: Via Santa Radegonda, 1, 20121 Milano MI | GPS: 45.4640° N, 9.1919° E)
- **Luini Panzerotti** (Address: Via Santa Radegonda, 16, 20121 Milano MI | GPS: 45.4642° N, 9.1920° E)

Photography Tips

Capture the spires at sunset for golden tones. Use a wide-angle lens for shots inside. Tripods are not allowed without prior permission.

Practical Information

Dress modestly; shoulders and knees must be covered. Bags may be checked for security.

Interesting Facts

- Construction began in 1386 and wasn't fully completed until 1965.
- It has over 3,400 statues, more than any other building in the world.

2. Galleria Vittorio Emanuele II

Overview

Italy's oldest shopping gallery, this 19th-century architectural gem is a masterpiece of glass, steel, and mosaic artistry. Its central dome creates an elegant meeting place for locals and tourists alike.

Why You Should Visit

Beyond luxury shopping, the gallery's architectural grandeur makes it a remarkable experience. The mosaic floor and arched ceiling are breathtaking.

Location

- Address: Piazza del Duomo, 20123 Milano MI, Italy
- GPS: 45.4659° N, 9.1916° E

Best Time to Visit

Evening hours are perfect for enjoying the lit-up dome.

Admission Tickets

Free entry.

How to Get There

Take the M1 or M3 line to Duomo Station, and the gallery is just steps away.

Hours of Opening

Open 24/7 for walking through, though shops follow their schedules (usually 10:00 AM - 8:00 PM).

Closest Town

Milan City Center

What to See and Do

- Stroll through the gallery and admire the mosaics.

- Visit iconic stores like Prada and Louis Vuitton.
- Spin on the mosaic bull for good luck (in the center of the floor).

Nearby Restaurants & Attractions

- **Camparino in Galleria** (Address: Piazza Duomo, 21, 20121 Milano MI | GPS: 45.4658° N, 9.1916° E)
- **Marchesi 1824** (Address: Via Santa Maria alla Porta, 11/a, 20123 Milano MI | GPS: 45.4659° N, 9.1915° E)

Photography Tips

Aim your lens upward to capture the dome's grandeur. Visit in the evening for reflections on the polished floor.

Practical Information

Be mindful of pickpockets, especially in crowded areas.

Interesting Facts

- Built in 1867, the gallery was designed by architect Giuseppe Mengoni.
- It's nicknamed Milan's "living room" due to its central role in city life.

3. Sforza Castle (Castello Sforzesco)

Overview

A 15th-century fortress turned cultural hub, Sforza Castle is a gateway to Milan's history. Its courtyards and museums display treasures from Renaissance art to ancient artifacts.

Why You Should Visit

The castle's rich history, impressive architecture, and diverse museum collections make it a treasure trove for history lovers.

Location

- Address: Piazza Castello, 20121 Milano MI, Italy
- GPS: 45.4709° N, 9.1798° E
  https://www.milanocastello.it

Best Time to Visit

Mid-morning or late afternoon to explore the grounds comfortably.

Admission Tickets

- Museum entry: €5
- Free entry to the courtyards

How to Get There

Metro: Take the M1 line to Cairoli Station. It's a short walk from there.

Hours of Opening

Tuesday-Sunday: 9:00 AM - 5:30 PM
Closed Mondays

Closest Town

Milan City Center

What to See and Do

- Visit the museums, including the Museum of Ancient Art.

- Stroll through the Sempione Park behind the castle.
- View Michelangelo's unfinished *Rondanini Pietà*.

Nearby Restaurants & Attractions

- **Il Salumaio di Montenapoleone** (Address: Via Santo Spirito, 10, 20121 Milano MI | GPS: 45.4700° N, 9.1795° E)
- **Terrazza Triennale** (Address: Viale Alemagna, 6, 20121 Milano MI | GPS: 45.4707° N, 9.1799° E)

Photography Tips

Position yourself at the entrance archway for a dramatic shot of the inner courtyard. Sunrise lighting creates beautiful shadows on the castle walls.

Practical Information

Wear comfortable shoes; the grounds are extensive. Some museums may have an additional fee.

Interesting Facts

- Leonardo da Vinci once worked here, designing defenses for the castle.
- The fortress has survived multiple sieges over centuries.

Northern Italy's landmarks speak to the enduring creativity of its people. These architectural icons promise an unforgettable journey into history and artistry.

Art and Fashion: The Last Supper, Contemporary Galleries, and Designer Boutiques

1. The Last Supper (Il Cenacolo)

- **Overview**
  Leonardo da Vinci's *The Last Supper* stands as one of the world's most iconic masterpieces. Housed within the refectory of Santa Maria delle Grazie, this Renaissance treasure draws art enthusiasts and history buffs alike for its unparalleled detail and emotional depth.
- **Why Visit:** Seeing *The Last Supper* in person offers an irreplaceable connection to one of the most transformative periods in art history. The experience is deeply moving and gives context to Leonardo's genius.
- **Location**
  Santa Maria delle Grazie, Piazza di Santa Maria delle Grazie, 2, 20123 Milano MI, Italy. **GPS:** 45.4662° N, 9.1705° E. **Website:**https://cenacolovinciano.org
- **Best Time to Visit:** Early morning reservations offer a quieter experience. Weekdays are generally less crowded than weekends.
- **Admission Tickets:** Tickets are approximately €15 and must be booked weeks in advance. Guided tours are available for additional fees.
- **How to Get There:** From Milan's central train station, take the M1 metro line to Cadorna and walk 10 minutes. Alternatively, tram lines 16 and 19 stop nearby.
- **Hours of Operation:** Tuesday–Sunday: 8:15 AM–7:00 PM. Closed on Mondays.
- **Closest Town:** Milan, Italy. Same as the location.

- **What to Do and See:** Explore the church of Santa Maria delle Grazie, a UNESCO World Heritage site. Don't miss the intricately designed cloister.
- **Best Nearby Restaurants and Attractions**
  - **Trattoria Milanese**, Via Santa Marta, 11, 20123 Milano MI, Italy. **GPS:** 45.4631° N, 9.1820° E.
  - **Sforza Castle (Castello Sforzesco)**, Piazza Castello, 20121 Milano MI, Italy. **GPS:** 45.4706° N, 9.1793° E.
- **Photography Tips:** Photography is prohibited to preserve the artwork. Take photos of the church exterior and surrounding gardens instead.
- **Laws/Rules**
  Strictly follow timed entry rules. Bags and cameras must be stored in lockers.
- **Practical Information:** Wear comfortable walking shoes. The visit lasts about 15 minutes, so arrive prepared for a short but impactful experience.
- **Interesting Facts:** The painting's condition has deteriorated over centuries due to Leonardo's experimental technique. Restoration efforts continue to this day.

2. Contemporary Art Galleries in Venice

- **Overview**
  Venice boasts cutting-edge contemporary art spaces such as the Peggy Guggenheim Collection, blending modern creations with Venice's timeless charm. These galleries challenge perceptions and push creative boundaries.
- **Why Visit:** Discover works by Picasso, Pollock, and Dalí alongside modern installations. The juxtaposition of old and new creates a thought-provoking experience.

- **Location:** Peggy Guggenheim Collection, Dorsoduro, 701-704, 30123 Venezia VE, Italy.
  - **GPS:** 45.4308° N, 12.3319° E.
  - **Website:** https://guggenheim-venice.it
- **Best Time to Visit:** Afternoons are quieter. Visit during the Biennale for added excitement.
- **Admission Tickets:** Entry costs around €15. Students and seniors can avail discounts.
- **How to Get There:** From Venice's Santa Lucia train station, take the vaporetto (water bus) Line 1 to the Accademia stop.
- **Hours of Operation:** Daily: 10:00 AM–6:00 PM. Closed Tuesdays.
- **Closest Town:** Venice, Italy. Same as the location.
- **What to Do and See:** Wander through Venice's Dorsoduro district, rich in bohemian energy and artisan shops.
- **Best Nearby Restaurants and Attractions**
  - **Osteria alle Testiere**, Calle del Mondo Novo, 5801, 30122 Venezia VE, Italy. GPS: 45.4355° N, 12.3408° E.
  - **Gallerie dell'Accademia**, Campo della Carità, 1050, 30123 Venezia VE, Italy. GPS: 45.4300° N, 12.3280° E.
- **Photography Tips:** Natural light is optimal in the sculpture garden. Avoid peak hours for clearer shots.
- **Laws/Rules**
  Large bags and flash photography are not allowed. Silence is encouraged inside galleries.
- **Practical Information:** Plan for at least two hours. Bring a guidebook or rent an audio tour for better context.
- **Interesting Facts:** Peggy Guggenheim's ashes are interred in the museum garden alongside her beloved dogs.

- **Overview**
  The Quadrilatero della Moda in Milan is synonymous with luxury shopping. Renowned brands like Prada, Versace, and Armani call this district home.
- **Why Visit:** Explore flagship stores, limited-edition collections, and cutting-edge fashion designs.
- **Location:** Via Monte Napoleone, 20121 Milano MI, Italy.
  - **GPS:** 45.4682° N, 9.1955° E.
- **Best Time to Visit:** Mornings and late afternoons are less crowded. Winter sales in January and July offer great deals.
- **Admission Tickets:** Free to explore; prices depend on your shopping budget.
- **How to Get There:** Take the M3 metro line to Montenapoleone Station.
- **Hours of Operation:** Most stores are open daily: 10:00 AM–7:30 PM.
- **Closest Town:** Milan, Italy. Same as the location.
- **What to Do and See:** Visit La Rinascente for a mix of high-end and emerging brands. Nearby, the Duomo di Milano offers a stunning architectural counterpoint.
- **Best Nearby Restaurants and Attractions**
  - **Nobu Milano**, Via Gastone Pisoni, 1, 20121 Milano MI, Italy.
    GPS: 45.4663° N, 9.1899° E.
  - **Teatro alla Scala**, Via Filodrammatici, 2, 20121 Milano MI, Italy.
    GPS: 45.4677° N, 9.1894° E.
- **Photography Tips:** Capture the elegance of Via Monte Napoleone at dusk when storefronts glow.

- **Laws/Rules**
  Some boutiques require appointments. Respect staff and merchandise.
- **Practical Information:** Wear comfortable yet stylish footwear. Be aware of pickpockets.
- **Interesting Facts:** Via Monte Napoleone is one of the most expensive streets in Europe, with a history dating back to Roman times.

These highlights showcase the rich interplay between art, culture, and fashion in Northern Italy, leaving every visitor inspired.

Milan's Culinary Scene: Aperitivo Culture, Local Markets, and Gourmet Dining

Milan is known for its vibrant food culture, where tradition meets innovation. Here are five culinary highlights to explore, complete with practical tips to make the most of your experience.

1. Aperitivo Culture: Navigli District

The Navigli District is synonymous with Milan's aperitivo culture. Aperitivo, akin to a pre-dinner ritual, pairs drinks with small bites like olives, focaccia, and cold cuts. Head to **Mag Café** for creative cocktails or **Spritz Navigli** for a relaxed vibe.

- **Location**: Naviglio Grande, Milan (GPS: 45.4498, 9.1713)
- **Contact**: +39 02 12345678 (Mag Café)
- **How to Get There**: Take Metro Line 2 (Green) to Porta Genova FS Station.
- **Opening Hours**: Typically 6 PM–9 PM.
- **Payment**: Cards and cash accepted.
- **Tips**: Italians dress smartly, so aim for casual elegance. No need to haggle; prices are fixed.

- **Language**: Basic Italian phrases like "Un aperitivo, per favore" (An aperitivo, please) can help.

2. Mercato Centrale Milano

This bustling market showcases fresh ingredients and artisan food stalls. Sample handmade pasta, aged cheeses, and regional desserts.

- **Location**: Piazza IV Novembre, 20124 Milan (GPS: 45.4856, 9.2033)
- **Contact**: +39 02 12345999
- **How to Get There**: Near Milano Centrale Station; accessible by Metro Line 2 or Line 3.
- **Opening Hours**: 8 AM–10 PM daily.
- **What to Shop For**: Truffle-infused products, balsamic vinegar, and local wines.
- **Payment**: Most vendors accept cards; bring cash for small purchases.
- **Safety**: Keep your belongings secure; pickpocketing can occur in busy areas.
- **Language**: Vendors often speak basic English.

3. Ristorante Cracco

For a high-end dining experience, Ristorante Cracco blends traditional Italian recipes with contemporary techniques. Try the saffron risotto or Milanese veal cutlet.

- **Location**: Galleria Vittorio Emanuele II, 20121 Milan (GPS: 45.4654, 9.1900)
- **Contact**: +39 02 876774
- **How to Get There**: Metro Line 1 to Duomo Station.
- **Opening Hours**: 12 PM–2:30 PM; 7 PM–11 PM. Closed Mondays.

- **Payment**: Cards preferred; reservations required.
- **Tips**: Dress formally and book weeks in advance.

4. Peck Milano

A gourmet paradise, Peck offers premium deli items, from cured meats to handmade chocolates. Perfect for gifts or a luxurious picnic.

- **Location**: Via Spadari 9, 20123 Milan (GPS: 45.4624, 9.1871)
- **Contact**: +39 02 8023161
- **How to Get There**: Metro Line 3 to Missori Station.
- **Opening Hours**: 9:30 AM–7:30 PM; closed Sundays.
- **What to Shop For**: Olive oil, panettone, and specialty pastas.
- **Tips**: Avoid bargaining; prices reflect quality.

5. Eataly Milano Smeraldo

Eataly combines dining, shopping, and education. Explore its three floors for freshly baked bread, regional wines, and cooking classes.

- **Location**: Piazza XXV Aprile 10, 20121 Milan (GPS: 45.4821, 9.1850)
- **Contact**: +39 02 49497301
- **How to Get There**: Metro Line 2 to Moscova Station.
- **Opening Hours**: 10 AM–11 PM daily.
- **What to Shop For**: Regional wines and artisanal pastas.
- **Payment**: Cards accepted.
- **Safety**: Busy but family-friendly.
- **Language**: Staff are fluent in English.

Milan's culinary adventures are best enjoyed with an open palate and a little local knowledge. Enjoy exploring this flavorful city!

Itinerary: Exploring Milan in Two Perfect Days

Milan, a city known for its vibrant energy and artistic legacy, is a fascinating mix of history and modernity. With just two days, you can experience its most iconic landmarks, savor its culinary delights, and soak in the lively atmosphere that makes it one of Italy's most dynamic destinations.

Day 1: The Classics and Local Life

Begin your Milanese adventure at the iconic **Duomo di Milano**, a magnificent Gothic cathedral that took centuries to complete. Arrive early to beat the crowds and take a tour of its interior before climbing to the rooftop terraces for a panoramic view of the city. The entrance fee is approximately €20 for rooftop access via elevator or €15 for the stairs.

Afterward, make your way to the nearby **Galleria Vittorio Emanuele II**, one of the world's oldest shopping galleries. Its impressive glass ceiling and high-end shops provide the perfect backdrop for a leisurely coffee break at **Caffè Biffi**, where a cappuccino costs around €5.

Next, walk to **Teatro alla Scala**, Milan's world-famous opera house. Opt for a guided tour of the museum for €9 or simply admire its façade. From there, explore **Brera**, an artistic district brimming with galleries, boutiques, and quaint trattorias. Enjoy a leisurely lunch at **Osteria di Brera**, with authentic risotto dishes priced between €15 and €20.

Spend your afternoon at the **Pinacoteca di Brera**, a renowned art museum housing works by Italian masters. Entry costs €15, and the collection provides a fascinating glimpse into the country's artistic heritage. Conclude your day with an aperitivo at **Navigli**, a canal-side area bustling with lively bars and restaurants. Aperitivo menus typically range from €10 to €15 per person.

Day 2: Modern Milan and Hidden Gems

On your second day, dive into the contemporary side of Milan. Start with a visit to **Santa Maria delle Grazie** to see Leonardo da Vinci's *The Last Supper*. Entry requires prior booking and costs €15. Following this, head to the nearby **Sforza Castle**, which houses multiple museums and is surrounded by lush gardens. Combined museum tickets cost €10.

For lunch, venture to the **Isola District**, known for its trendy vibe and local eateries. Sample classic Milanese dishes at **Trattoria Bertamè**, where main courses cost around €18. Afterward, explore **Bosco Verticale**, the "Vertical Forest," an architectural marvel covered in greenery.

Wrap up your trip at **Fondazione Prada**, a modern art museum offering an array of thought-provoking exhibitions. Admission is €15, and it's an excellent spot to reflect on Milan's innovative spirit. Finish your evening with dinner at **Al Pont de Ferr**, an award-winning restaurant along the Navigli, with a tasting menu starting at €70.

Estimated Budget for Two Days in Milan:

- Accommodation (mid-range hotel): €150 per night
- Food and drinks: €100 per day
- Attractions: €90 total
- Transportation (metro and trams): €15 total
- **Total: €505 per person**

Guatemala, a country rich in culture and breathtaking landscapes, offers an exciting blend of ancient ruins, vibrant markets, and natural wonders. This itinerary balances must-see sights with authentic experiences, ensuring an unforgettable journey.

Day 1-2: Antigua's Historic Charm

Start your adventure in **Antigua**, a UNESCO World Heritage Site. Explore its cobblestone streets, colorful facades, and historical landmarks like **Santa Catalina Arch** and **La Merced Church**. Spend time at the bustling **Central Market** and enjoy traditional Guatemalan dishes such as pepián at **Café Condesa**, where meals average $10.

For an active morning, hike up **Cerro de la Cruz** for panoramic views of the city. Accommodation in Antigua ranges from $40 to $100 per night for boutique hotels. Transportation via shuttles or tuk-tuks costs around $5 per trip.

Day 3-4: Lake Atitlán and Surrounding Villages

Travel to **Lake Atitlán**, a stunning volcanic lake surrounded by charming villages. Stay in **Panajachel** and use it as a base to explore nearby towns like **San Juan La Laguna**, known for its art cooperatives and coffee tours. Boat rides between villages cost $3 to $5 each way.

Visit **San Pedro La Laguna** for a short hike up **Indian Nose**, which offers spectacular sunrise views. Guided tours cost about $25. Enjoy fresh tilapia or traditional tacos at **Restaurante El Barrio**, where meals range from $8 to $12.

Day 5-6: Chichicastenango Market and Mayan Ruins

Head to **Chichicastenango**, home to one of the largest open-air markets in Central America. Shop for handcrafted textiles, pottery, and wooden masks while enjoying the vibrant local culture. Make sure to visit **Santo Tomás Church**, a blend of Mayan and Catholic traditions.

Next, journey to **Tikal National Park**, one of the most impressive Mayan archaeological sites. Entry costs $20, and guided tours average $35. Stay overnight in nearby **Flores**, a quaint island town where mid-range hotels cost around $60 per night.

Day 7: Semuc Champey's Natural Beauty

Conclude your trip with a visit to **Semuc Champey**, a series of turquoise pools surrounded by lush jungle. Guided tours from **Lanquin** cost around $60 and include transportation, lunch, and park entrance fees. This natural wonder is perfect for a relaxing swim or an adventurous hike to the viewpoint.

Estimated Budget for a Week in Guatemala:

- Accommodation (mid-range): $50 per night
- Food and drinks: $20 per day
- Transportation (shuttles and boats): $100 total
- Attractions and guided tours: $200 total
- **Total: $750 per person**

Chapter 5: Venice – A City of Timeless Romance

Venice is a city that stirs the imagination with its art, history, and timeless beauty. From the grandeur of St. Mark's Basilica to the lively Rialto Bridge, every corner tells a story. Glide through serene canals, wander vibrant islands, and savor three unforgettable days immersed in Venice's unforgettable charm.

Iconic Landmarks: St. Mark's Basilica, Doge's Palace, and Rialto Bridge

1. St. Mark's Basilica, Venice

Overview

St. Mark's Basilica is a masterpiece of Byzantine architecture and a centerpiece of Venice's storied history. With its shimmering mosaics, opulent domes, and intricate details, it reflects centuries of art and devotion. Known locally as the Basilica di San Marco, it's one of Italy's most treasured landmarks, drawing visitors from around the world.

Why Visit

It's a feast for the senses—golden mosaics depict biblical tales, marble floors feel like walking on art, and the interior exudes timeless reverence. Visitors can climb to the terrace for breathtaking views of Piazza San Marco and the Venetian Lagoon.

Location

- Piazza San Marco, 328, 30124 Venice VE, Italy
- GPS: 45.4340° N, 12.3396° E
  https://www.basilicasanmarco.it/

Best Time to Visit

Early mornings in spring or autumn offer cooler weather and fewer crowds. Midweek visits are ideal for a more serene experience.

Admission Tickets

Basic entry is free, but specific areas like the museum or Pala d'Oro altar require tickets (approx. €5–€10).

How to Get There

From Venice's Santa Lucia train station, take Vaporetto Line 1 or 2 to the San Marco stop.

Hours of Operation

9:30 AM – 5:15 PM, with shorter hours on Sundays and holidays.

Closest Town

Venice (Santa Croce neighborhood: Piazzale Roma, GPS: 45.4372° N, 12.3215° E)

What to Do and See

Admire the Basilica's dazzling mosaics, climb to the museum and terrace, and visit the treasury's religious artifacts.

Nearby Restaurants and Attractions

- **Quadri Alajmo Restaurant**: Piazza San Marco, 121, Venice, GPS: 45.4338° N, 12.3383° E
- **T Fondaco dei Tedeschi Rooftop**: Calle del Fontego dei Tedeschi, GPS: 45.4386° N, 12.3366° E

Photography Tips

Morning light enhances the mosaics. Photos are prohibited inside, but the terrace offers postcard-worthy shots.

Practical Information

Large bags aren't allowed inside, and modest attire is required.

Interesting Fact

The basilica was built in 828 to house the relics of St. Mark, smuggled out of Alexandria by Venetian merchants.

2. Doge's Palace, Venice

Overview
The Doge's Palace is an architectural gem that served as the residence of Venice's rulers and the center of its political life. Its Gothic design, grand halls, and Bridge of Sighs make it an iconic part of Venetian history.

Why Visit

Step into the past by exploring its grand chambers, secret prisons, and ornate frescoes by Venetian masters like Tintoretto and Veronese.

Location

- o   Piazza San Marco, 1, 30124 Venice VE, Italy
- o   GPS: 45.4339°   N,   12.3400°   E

Best Time to Visit

Late afternoons in winter provide a quieter experience and atmospheric lighting.

Admission Tickets

Tickets start at €25 for standard entry, including access to museum exhibits.

How to Get There

Accessible via Vaporetto Line 1 or 2 to the San Marco stop.

Hours of Operation

9:00 AM – 7:00 PM, with last admission an hour before closing.

Closest Town

Venice (Cannaregio neighborhood: Rio Terà Lista di Spagna, GPS: 45.4412° N, 12.3211° E)

What to Do and See

Walk through the Hall of the Great Council, cross the Bridge of Sighs, and explore the dungeons.

Nearby Restaurants and Attractions

- **Antico Pignolo**: Calle Specchieri, 451, GPS: 45.4345° N, 12.3398° E
- **Teatro La Fenice**: Campo San Fantin, GPS: 45.4335° N, 12.3348° E

Photography Tips

Capture the façade during sunset when the light highlights the intricate details.

Practical Information

Strollers and large backpacks must be checked at the entrance.

Interesting Fact

The palace once held Casanova, who famously escaped from its prison cells in 1756.

3. Rialto Bridge, Venice

Overview
The Rialto Bridge is the oldest and most iconic bridge crossing Venice's Grand Canal. Built in the late 16th century, it's both a practical crossing and a symbol of Venice's architectural ingenuity.

Why Visit

It's a spot to marvel at Venice's vibrant canals, enjoy shopping at boutique stalls, and watch gondoliers navigate the waterways below.

Location

- Sestiere San Polo, 30125 Venice VE, Italy
- GPS: 45.4381° N, 12.3358° E

Best Time to Visit

Evenings during the golden hour provide magical views of the illuminated canal.

Admission Tickets

Free to access, though nearby tours may have costs.

How to Get There

Walk from the San Marco area (10 minutes) or take Vaporetto Line 1 to the Rialto stop.

Hours of Operation

Open 24 hours.

Closest Town

Venice (San Polo neighborhood: Campo San Polo, GPS: 45.4389° N, 12.3289° E)

What to Do and See

Shop for souvenirs, enjoy gelato from nearby vendors, and soak in the canal views.

Nearby Restaurants and Attractions

- **Trattoria Antiche Carampane**: Calle dei Carampane, GPS: 45.4375° N, 12.3282° E
- **Rialto Market**: Campo de la Pescaria, GPS: 45.4387° N, 12.3365° E

Photography Tips

Shoot from the opposite bank for a full view of the bridge or from the bridge itself for dynamic canal shots.

Practical Information

Crowds are common; visit early or late for a quieter experience.

Interesting Fact

The original wooden bridge collapsed multiple times before the current stone version was completed in 1591.

These landmarks offer more than historical intrigue—they're a glimpse into the heart of Northern Italy's culture and creativity. Plan wisely to make your journey memorabl.

Exploring the Canals: Gondolas, Water Taxis, and Hidden Corners

Northern Italy's canals offer a timeless experience, transporting visitors into a world shaped by history and Venetian charm. The serene waters are best navigated by gondolas and water taxis, but there's much more than the postcard-perfect scenes. Hidden corners, quiet alleyways, and secret gardens bring a sense of adventure to your exploration.

Best Places for Outdoor Adventures

Start your journey in Venice's Grand Canal, the centerpiece of this unique city. Water taxis provide quick access to landmarks like the Rialto Bridge and St. Mark's Basilica. For a quieter experience, head to Cannaregio, where smaller canals meander through lesser-known neighborhoods, offering a slower pace. The island of Burano, famous for colorful houses, and Torcello, rich in medieval history, make for delightful day trips.

Brief Overview and Costs

A gondola ride typically costs around €80 for a 30-minute journey, increasing to €100 after sunset. Water taxis are pricier, starting at €15-

20 per person for short trips, but they're convenient for traveling to multiple destinations. Public water buses (vaporettos) are economical, with day passes starting at €25.

Seasonal Considerations

Spring and early autumn are ideal for visiting, offering mild weather and fewer crowds. Summer can bring high humidity and a flood of tourists, while winter provides a misty, atmospheric charm. Keep in mind that canal flooding, or acqua alta, may affect access in late autumn and winter.

Safety Tips and Guidelines

Wear comfortable shoes for walking and stepping into gondolas or taxis. Keep personal belongings secure, as crowds can attract pickpockets. Life jackets aren't mandatory on gondolas but are available on water taxis—ask if you're concerned. Always check water levels, especially during acqua alta.

Permits, Difficulty Level, and Expected Duration

No permits are required for casual canal exploration. Gondola rides are effortless, suitable for all ages. Water taxi rides range from 10 minutes to an hour, depending on your itinerary.

Packing List

Pack a light jacket for cooler evenings, sunscreen for sunny days, and waterproof footwear for unexpected splashes. Bring a reusable water bottle to stay hydrated.

Help protect Venice's fragile ecosystem by avoiding single-use plastics. Opt for eco-friendly operators when possible and respect the city's no-swimming policy in canals.

For emergencies, dial 112. Venice's main hospital is Ospedale SS Giovanni e Paolo (phone: +39 041 5294111).

- **Row Venice**: Offers traditional rowing tours.
  Website:http://www.rowvenice.org
- **Venice Free Walking Tour**: Great for guided walks combined with canal history.
  Website:http://www.venicefreewalkingtour.com

Prepare for a journey that combines relaxation, adventure, and an intimate glimpse into Venice's timeless waterways.

Island Excursions: Murano, Burano, and Torcello

1. Murano

Overview:
Murano, a short boat ride from Venice, is synonymous with masterful glassmaking. This island has been at the center of Venetian artistry for centuries and brims with workshops, galleries, and historical landmarks. It's a blend of craftsmanship and history that feels alive as you stroll its canals.

Why You Should Visit:

Murano is a haven for art lovers and history buffs. Its glassmaking tradition, dating back to the 13th century, continues to inspire awe. Watch artisans shape molten glass into exquisite art pieces or explore museums showcasing centuries-old craftsmanship.

Location:

- Murano Island, Venice Lagoon, Italy
- **GPS:** 45.4570° N, 12.3538° E
- https://muranoglassitaly.com/

Best Time to Visit:

Late spring to early autumn (April–September) when the weather is pleasant and the glass furnaces are active.

Admission Tickets:

Most glassblowing demonstrations are free, but museum entry fees range from €8–€12.

How to Get There:

From Venice, take Vaporetto Line 4.1 or 4.2 from Fondamenta Nove or San Zaccaria. The ride takes about 15 minutes.

Hours of Opening:

Shops and studios typically open between 9:30 AM and 6:00 PM. The Museo del Vetro (Glass Museum) is open from 10:00 AM to 5:00 PM.

Closest Town:

- o Venice (Piazza San Marco)
- o **Location:** Piazza San Marco, 30124 Venice, Italy
- o **GPS:** 45.4340° N, 12.3388° E

What to Do and See:

- Visit the Museo del Vetro to explore the history of glassmaking.
- Watch live glassblowing demonstrations at local workshops.
- Admire the 12th-century Church of Santa Maria e San Donato.

Nearby Restaurants & Attractions:

- **Trattoria Busa alla Torre da Lele** (Riva Longa, 18, 30141 Murano, Italy; **GPS:** 45.4575° N, 12.3530° E) for seafood dishes.
- **Venice Murano Lighthouse** for panoramic views.

Photography Tips:

Capture glassmakers in action with natural light. Early mornings offer softer lighting along the canals.

Laws/Rules:
Respect workshops by not touching glass displays. Many areas prohibit photography during demonstrations.

Practical Information:

Shops may close for siestas between 1:00–3:00 PM, so plan visits accordingly.

Interesting Facts:

- Murano glass was originally moved from Venice in the 13th century to reduce fire hazards in the city.
- The island has its own glassmaking guilds to protect trade secrets.

2. Burano

Overview:
Burano stands out for its vibrant houses and delicate lace artistry. This fisherman's island is a kaleidoscope of colors and charm, making it a photographer's dream.

Why You Should Visit:

Known for its lace-making heritage and vibrant streets, Burano offers a glimpse into traditional Venetian life. The colors of the houses are said to help fishermen find their way home through the lagoon's fog.

Location:

- Burano Island, Venice Lagoon, Italy
- **GPS:** 45.4852° N, 12.4162° E
- https://www.visitvenezia.eu/

Best Time to Visit:

Weekdays during late spring for fewer crowds and optimal lighting.

Admission Tickets:

Free to wander, but lace museum fees are around €5.

How to Get There:

Vaporetto Line 12 from Fondamenta Nove, Venice, takes about 45 minutes.

Hours of Opening:

Shops open from 9:30 AM to 6:30 PM. Museo del Merletto (Lace Museum) operates 10:00 AM to 5:00 PM.

Closest Town:

- o   Venice
- o   **Location:** Piazza San Marco, 30124 Venice, Italy
- o   **GPS:** 45.4340° N, 12.3388° E

What to Do and See:

- Explore Museo del Merletto to learn about lace-making traditions.
- Stroll along Via Baldassarre Galuppi, lined with shops and cafes.

Nearby Restaurants & Attractions:

- **Trattoria al Gatto Nero** (Via Giudecca, 88, 30142 Burano, Italy; **GPS:** 45.4853° N, 12.4175° E) serves classic Venetian dishes.
- **Tre Ponti Bridge** for stunning canal views.

Photography Tips:

Capture house reflections in the canals during the golden hour. Wide-angle lenses work well here.

Laws/Rules:
Avoid entering private courtyards unless invited. Local laws prohibit drone usage without permits.

Practical Information:

Burano is walkable, so wear comfortable shoes for cobblestone streets.

Interesting Facts:

- Legend says the bright colors helped fishermen spot their homes through thick fog.
- Burano lace has been prized since the 16th century.

3. Torcello

Overview:
Torcello is a peaceful retreat, home to some of Venice's oldest monuments. Its quiet charm and lush greenery contrast the busier islands.

Why You Should Visit:

Torcello offers serenity and history. It's home to the Cathedral of Santa Maria Assunta, with its 11th-century mosaics, and the mysterious Throne of Attila.

Location:

- Torcello Island, Venice Lagoon, Italy
- **GPS:** 45.4884° N, 12.4174° E
- https://www.visitvenezia.eu/

Best Time to Visit:

Spring or fall for fewer crowds and cooler weather.

Admission Tickets:

Entry to the cathedral is €5.

How to Get There:

Take Vaporetto Line 12 from Burano (10 minutes) or Venice (50 minutes).

Hours of Opening:

The cathedral opens from 10:30 AM to 5:00 PM.

Closest Town:

- o Burano
- o **Location:** Via Baldassarre Galuppi, 30142 Burano, Italy
- o **GPS:** 45.4852° N, 12.4162° E

What to Do and See:

- Admire Byzantine mosaics at the cathedral.
- Walk through the quiet paths to the Devil's Bridge.

Nearby Restaurants & Attractions:

- **Locanda Cipriani** (Piazza Santa Fosca, 29, 30142 Torcello, Italy; **GPS:** 45.4875° N, 12.4168° E) for a refined dining experience.

Photography Tips:

Capture mosaic details in the cathedral during midday for even lighting.

Laws/Rules:

Be respectful in the cathedral—no flash photography. Maintain quiet in religious areas.

Practical Information:

Bring cash; many small vendors do not accept cards.

Interesting Facts:

- Torcello was one of the first Venetian islands to be settled, dating back to the 5th century.
- Ernest Hemingway spent time here, writing portions of *Across the River and Into the Trees.*

These three islands together offer a slice of Northern Italy's rich lagoon history, art, and culture.

Itinerary: A 3-Day Experience of Venice and Its Surroundings

Venice, a city like no other, captivates visitors with its labyrinth of canals, grand piazzas, and intricate architecture. In three days, you can immerse yourself in the essence of this iconic destination and its nearby treasures. This itinerary will guide you through a thoughtfully curated plan for an unforgettable journey.

Day 1: Exploring the Heart of Venice

Start your day in **Piazza San Marco**, often called the soul of Venice. Visit **St. Mark's Basilica**, where its golden mosaics and Byzantine design will leave you mesmerized. Entry to the basilica is free, but access to the museum costs around €7. Then, climb the **Campanile di San Marco** for panoramic views of the city (€10).

From there, take a leisurely stroll to the **Doge's Palace**. The palace's halls, adorned with historical frescoes, offer a glimpse into Venice's past (€25 with skip-the-line access). Don't miss the **Bridge of Sighs**, where whispers of centuries-old stories linger.

For lunch, head to **Trattoria al Gatto Nero** on the nearby island of Burano. Famous for its seafood risotto, the meal will cost you about €40 per person, including wine. Spend your afternoon wandering Burano's vibrant streets and admire the craftsmanship of its lace-making artisans.

As the sun sets, return to Venice and hop on a **gondola ride** for a serene experience through the canals. Prices start at €80 for 30 minutes. End your day with a dinner of Venetian cicchetti (small bites) at **Osteria Bancogiro** (€30 per person).

Day 2: Hidden Gems and Local Life

Begin your day in the **Cannaregio district**, home to the **Jewish Ghetto**—an area rich in culture and history. Stroll through its quiet streets and visit the Jewish Museum (€10).

Next, take a vaporetto (water bus) to **Murano**, renowned for its glassblowing workshops. Stop at the **Murano Glass Museum** (€10) to understand the artistry behind this centuries-old craft. You can also purchase souvenirs directly from artisans, with prices ranging from €20 to €100 depending on the item.

For lunch, enjoy a traditional Venetian meal at **Trattoria da Jonny** (€35 per person). In the afternoon, explore **San Giorgio Maggiore**, an island known for its peaceful ambiance. The climb up the bell tower (€6) rewards you with a stunning view of Venice's skyline.

As evening approaches, take a private boat tour through the **Venetian Lagoon** to witness the city's beauty under twilight (€120 per group). Conclude your day with a fine dining experience at **Antiche Carampane**, known for its fresh seafood and impeccable service (€70 per person).

Day 3: Art, Culture, and Surrounding Beauty

Dedicate your final day to Venice's art and cultural scene. Start with the **Peggy Guggenheim Collection**, where modern art lovers can admire works by Picasso, Pollock, and Dalí (€15). Then, move on to the **Accademia Gallery**, which houses masterpieces from Venetian artists like Titian and Tintoretto (€12).

For lunch, enjoy the lively atmosphere at **Osteria alle Testiere** (€45 per person). Afterward, venture to **Giudecca Island**, known for its quiet charm and incredible views of the city. Relax at **Hilton Molino Stucky's Skyline Rooftop Bar** with a cocktail in hand (€15).

Wrap up your Venice trip with a sunset view from the **Rialto Bridge** and an authentic Italian dinner at **Ristorante Quadri** overlooking Piazza San Marco (€90 per person).

Estimated Budget for 3 Days in Venice:

- Accommodation (3 nights in a mid-range hotel): €400
- Meals (lunches, dinners, snacks): €300
- Attractions and tours: €170
- Transportation (vaporetto, gondola, private boat): €150
- Souvenirs and extras: €50

- **Total:** Approximately €1,070 per person

A Complete Exploration of Guatemala's Best

Guatemala is a land of vibrant landscapes, ancient ruins, and warm hospitality. With careful planning, you can uncover some of the country's most iconic spots while staying within a reasonable budget.

Day 1: Antigua

Start your journey in **Antigua**, a UNESCO World Heritage site brimming with colonial charm. Begin your morning with a coffee tour at **Finca Filadelfia** (€25) to learn about the region's prized beans. Then, explore **Santa Catalina Arch**, a historic landmark, and the ruins of **La Merced Church**.

For lunch, try local specialties like pepian (a traditional stew) at **La Fonda de la Calle Real** (€15 per person). In the afternoon, hike up **Cerro de la Cruz** for panoramic views of the city and surrounding volcanoes.

Spend your evening at **Café Sky**, a rooftop bar with a lively atmosphere and affordable meals (€20 per person). Accommodation options like **Hotel Casa Santo Domingo** offer mid-range comfort at €80 per night.

Day 2: Lake Atitlán

Head to **Lake Atitlán**, often described as one of the most beautiful lakes in the world. Start with a scenic boat ride (€15) to explore the villages surrounding the lake, such as **San Juan la Laguna** and **Santiago Atitlán**, known for their local art and traditional weaving.

Have lunch in **Panajachel** at **Café Loco**, where the coffee and avocado toast come highly recommended (€12 per person). Spend your afternoon kayaking or taking a swim in the crystal-clear waters (€10 for kayak rental).

For dinner, visit **Circus Bar**, a quirky spot known for its pizzas and live music (€25 per person). Stay overnight at a lakeside eco-lodge like **Casa del Mundo** (€70 per night).

Day 3: Tikal National Park

On your final day, take an early flight or bus to **Tikal National Park**, home to ancient Mayan ruins set within a lush jungle. Entry costs approximately €20, with guided tours available for €30. Explore the towering pyramids, temples, and wildlife, including howler monkeys and colorful toucans.

Lunch is available at the park's on-site restaurant (€15). Spend the afternoon exploring the surrounding trails or relaxing in the tranquility of the jungle.

If time permits, return to Guatemala City and enjoy a farewell dinner at **El Portal**, a restaurant famous for its authentic Guatemalan dishes (€30 per person).

Estimated Budget for Guatemala Trip:

- Accommodation (3 nights in mid-range hotels): €230
- Meals (breakfasts, lunches, dinners): €150
- Attractions and activities: €120
- Transportation (boat rides, buses, flights): €200
- Souvenirs and extras: €50

- **Total:** Approximately **€750** per person

Both Venice and Guatemala provide incredible experiences, each offering a distinctive atmosphere and activities. With well-planned itineraries, you can make the most of your vacation while staying within budget.

Chapter 6: The Lakes of Northern Italy – Serenity and Splendor

Northern Italy's lakes are a treasure trove of beauty and relaxation, each offering its own character and charm. From the elegant villas of Lake Como to the family-friendly shores of Lake Garda and the historic gems around Lake Maggiore, this chapter leads you through an unforgettable 3-day journey filled with wonder.

Lake Como: Bellagio, Varenna, and Luxurious Villas

1. Bellagio

Overview
Bellagio, often called the "Pearl of Lake Como," boasts cobbled streets, panoramic lake views, and an irresistible old-world charm. Its strategic position at the meeting point of the lake's two branches makes it a favored spot for breathtaking vistas and peaceful strolls.

Why Visit

This lakeside town offers an authentic Italian ambiance, with quaint boutiques, waterfront cafes, and some of the best gelato spots in Northern Italy. The manicured gardens of Villa Melzi are perfect for leisurely exploration.

Location & GPS

- o Bellagio, Province of Como, Italy
- o GPS: 45.9876° N, 9.2612° E

Official Website

http://www.bellagiolakecomo.com

Best Time to Visit

April to October for warmer weather and blooming gardens.

Admission Tickets

Villa Melzi Gardens: €8. Open daily from 10:00 AM to 6:30 PM.

How to Get There

From Milan: Take a train to Varenna, then a ferry across to Bellagio. Alternatively, drive 1.5 hours via SS36.

Closest Town

- Lecco (24 km)
- GPS: 45.8579° N, 9.3988° E

What to See and Do

- Stroll the lakefront promenade.
- Visit the neo-classical Villa Melzi.
- Explore quaint shops and artisan stores.

Best Nearby Restaurants & Attractions

- **Trattoria San Giacomo** (Via Centrale 1, GPS: 45.9863° N, 9.2610° E)
- **Villa Serbelloni Gardens** (Via Roma 1, GPS: 45.9885° N, 9.2591° E)

Photography Tips

Capture the reflection of the Alps on the lake during the golden hour. Focus on details like flower-laden balconies and narrow alleys.

Rules

No swimming near ferry docks. Respect private property boundaries.

Practical Information

Bellagio can get crowded in summer. Arrive early to avoid peak tourist hours.

Interesting Fact

Bellagio inspired the name of the famed Bellagio Hotel in Las Vegas

2. Varenna

Overview

A picturesque fishing village on the eastern shore of Lake Como, Varenna combines natural beauty with centuries-old architecture. Its vibrant houses and serene waterfront are a visual delight.

Why Visit

Varenna offers tranquility and authenticity. It's home to the romantic Villa Monastero and the scenic Lovers' Walk (Passeggiata degli Innamorati), which hugs the lakefront.

Location & GPS

- o   Varenna, Province of Lecco, Italy
- o   GPS: 46.0116° N, 9.2832° E

Official Website: http://www.varennaitaly.com

Best Time to Visit

Spring and autumn for fewer crowds and pleasant temperatures.

Admission Tickets

Villa Monastero: €10. Open daily from 9:00 AM to 6:00 PM.

How to Get There

From Milan: Train to Varenna-Esino station, a short walk to the village.

Closest Town

- o Bellano (4 km)
- o GPS: 46.0595° N, 9.3088° E

What to See and Do

- Walk the Lovers' Walk.
- Visit the botanical gardens of Villa Monastero.
- Stop by Castello di Vezio, a hilltop castle with panoramic views.

Best Nearby Restaurants & Attractions

- **Al Prato** (Piazza San Giorgio 5, GPS: 46.0125° N, 9.2831° E)
- **Ristorante La Vista** (Via XX Settembre 35, GPS: 46.0128° N, 9.2836° E)

Photography Tips

Capture reflections of Varenna's colorful houses in the lake during early morning. The Lovers' Walk is perfect for romantic snapshots.

Rules
Drone usage is restricted. Respect the quiet atmosphere.

Practical Information

Wear comfortable shoes for steep paths and stairs.

Interesting Fact

Varenna is one of the few Lake Como towns that retain its medieval layout.

3. Luxurious Villas

Overview

Lake Como's villas are synonymous with elegance, blending Renaissance architecture and lush gardens. Highlights include Villa Carlotta, Villa del Balbianello, and Villa Monastero.

Why Visit

These villas are masterpieces of architecture and landscaping, offering insight into the region's aristocratic past.

Location & GPS

- **Villa Carlotta**: Tremezzo, GPS: 45.9845° N, 9.2232° E
- **Villa del Balbianello**: Lenno, GPS: 45.9668° N, 9.1920° E

Official Websites

- Villa Carlotta:http://www.villacarlotta.it
- Villa del Balbianello:http://www.fondoambiente.it

Best Time to Visit

Spring for blooming gardens; autumn for fewer tourists.

Admission Tickets

- Villa Carlotta: €12. Open daily from 9:00 AM to 7:30 PM.
- Villa del Balbianello: €10 for gardens, €20 for guided tours. Open Tuesday-Sunday, 10:00 AM to 6:00 PM.

How to Get There

- Villa Carlotta: Accessible via ferry from Bellagio or drive via SP583.
- Villa del Balbianello: Ferry to Lenno, then a 20-minute walk or water taxi.

Closest Towns

- Tremezzo (Villa Carlotta): GPS: 45.9928° N, 9.2247° E
- Lenno (Villa del Balbianello): GPS: 45.9661° N, 9.1932° E

What to See and Do

- Explore lush gardens.
- Admire art collections at Villa Carlotta.
- Take a guided tour of Villa del Balbianello's interior.

Best Nearby Restaurants & Attractions

- **La Darsena** (Via Regina 3, GPS: 45.9915° N, 9.2307° E)
- **Al Veluu Ristorante** (Via Rogaro 11, GPS: 45.9852° N, 9.2248° E)

Photography Tips

Sunrise and sunset provide the best light for capturing villas against the lake.

Rules
No flash photography indoors. Gardens have designated pathways.

Practical Information

Plan visits during weekdays to avoid crowds.

Interesting Fact

Villa del Balbianello featured in *Star Wars: Episode II* and *Casino Royale*.

These highlights ensure an unforgettable trip to Lake Como, blending culture, relaxation, and awe-inspiring views.

Lake Garda: Adventure, Family Fun, and Sirmione's History

1. Sirmione's Scaliger Castle

Overview:
Sirmione's Scaliger Castle is a medieval fortress standing tall by Lake Garda. It offers visitors a chance to experience history through its well-preserved walls, breathtaking lake views, and ancient architecture. A walk through its narrow passageways feels like a journey back in time.

Why You Should Visit:

This castle isn't just a historical site; it's a doorway to understanding the stories of old Italian life while enjoying panoramic views of Lake Garda from the tower. Families and history enthusiasts will appreciate its timeless charm.

- o **Location:** Piazza Castello, 34, 25019 Sirmione BS, Italy. GPS: 45.4939° N, 10.6069° E
- o https://www.sirmionecastle.it

Best Time to Visit: Late spring and early autumn provide pleasant weather and fewer crowds.

Admission Tickets: Adults €6, reduced €3 for EU citizens aged 18-25. Free for children under 18.

How to Get There: From Desenzano del Garda train station, take a bus to Sirmione. If driving, parking is available nearby at Viale Marconi.

Hours of Opening:

- o   Tuesday to Sunday: 9:00 AM – 5:00 PM
- o   Closed on Mondays.

Closest Town: Desenzano del Garda. Address: Piazza Malvezzi, 25015 Desenzano BS, Italy. GPS: 45.4716° N, 10.5372° E

What to Do and See:

- Climb the tower for stunning lake views.
- Explore the drawbridge and walk along the walls.
- Visit nearby Grotte di Catullo, an ancient Roman villa.

Best Nearby Restaurants & Attractions:

- **La Speranzina**: Elegant dining with lake views. Address: Via Dante, 16, Sirmione BS. GPS: 45.4914° N, 10.6073° E
- **Spiaggia Grifone**: A relaxing lakeside beach for swimming. Address: Lungolago Armando Diaz, Sirmione BS. GPS: 45.4950° N, 10.6042° E

Photography Tips: The morning light illuminates the castle beautifully, especially from the lakeside. Sunset shots from the tower are spectacular.

Laws/Rules:

- Drones are not permitted.

- Stay on designated paths for safety.

Practical Information: Wear sturdy shoes for climbing stairs. Parking in Sirmione can be challenging; arrive early.

Interesting Facts: The castle is surrounded by water, making it one of Italy's rare fortresses with such a setting.

2. Gardaland Theme Park

Overview:
Gardaland, Italy's premier amusement park, blends thrilling rides with immersive family experiences. Situated on Lake Garda's southern shores, it's perfect for visitors of all ages.

Why You Should Visit:

It's not just about roller coasters; Gardaland offers something entertaining for the entire family, from themed attractions to water rides and live shows.

- **Location:** Via Derna, 4, 37014 Castelnuovo del Garda VR, Italy. GPS: 45.4501° N, 10.7195° E
- https://www.gardaland.it

Best Time to Visit: Weekdays in spring or early fall are less crowded.

Admission Tickets: Tickets start at €35. Online discounts available.

How to Get There: From Peschiera del Garda train station, a shuttle bus runs directly to the park.

Hours of Opening: Hours vary; check the website for details. Typically, 10:00 AM – 6:00 PM.

Closest Town: Peschiera del Garda. Address: Piazza Ferdinando di Savoia, 37019 VR, Italy. GPS: 45.4398° N, 10.6873° E

What to Do and See:

- Ride the adrenaline-pumping Raptor roller coaster.
- Explore Peppa Pig Land for younger children.
- Enjoy the Sea Life Aquarium adjacent to the park.

Best Nearby Restaurants & Attractions:

- **Trattoria Bella Italia**: Authentic Italian cuisine. Address: Via Venezia, 74, Peschiera del Garda. GPS: 45.4382° N, 10.6901° E
- **Lido Cappuccini**: A peaceful lakeside spot for a swim. Address: Str. Bergamini, 37019 VR. GPS: 45.4427° N, 10.7026° E

Photography Tips: Capture the rides against the backdrop of Lake Garda. Snap candid shots at sunset for vibrant colors.

Laws/Rules:

- Height restrictions apply for some rides.
- Large bags must be stored in lockers.

Practical Information: Dress comfortably and bring sunscreen. Purchase tickets online to avoid long queues.

Interesting Facts: Gardaland ranks among the top ten amusement parks in Europe.

3. Monte Baldo Cable Car

Overview:

The Monte Baldo cable car offers a ride to panoramic views of Lake Garda and the surrounding mountains, creating a perfect adventure for nature lovers and photographers.

Why You Should Visit:

It's an unforgettable way to witness Lake Garda from above, with hiking trails and wildflower-strewn meadows at the top.

- **Location:** Via Monte Baldo, 12, 37018 Malcesine VR, Italy. GPS: 45.7623° N, 10.8084° E
- https://www.funiviedelbaldo.it

Best Time to Visit: Late spring to autumn for clear skies and open trails.

Admission Tickets: Round-trip tickets: €25 for adults, €15 for children.

How to Get There: Malcesine is accessible by ferry or car. Ample parking near the cable car station.

Hours of Opening: Vary by season. Summer: 8:00 AM – 6:00 PM.

Closest Town: Malcesine. Address: Piazza Statuto, 37018 VR, Italy. GPS: 45.7626° N, 10.8113° E

What to Do and See:

- Hike scenic trails at the summit.
- Stop at Rifugio Monte Baldo for local dishes.

Best Nearby Restaurants & Attractions:

- **Al Torchio**: Cozy trattoria with traditional fare. Address: Via Gardesana, 4, Malcesine. GPS: 45.7632° N, 10.8121° E
- **Malcesine Castle**: A historic site with amazing views. Address: Via Castello, 37018 VR. GPS: 45.7629° N, 10.8132° E

Photography Tips: The rotating cabins allow 360-degree shots during the ride. Capture the lake's reflection on clear days.

Laws/Rules:

- Stay within marked hiking paths.
- No littering; bins are available.

Practical Information: Bring layers; it can get chilly at higher altitudes.

Interesting Facts: The cable car rotates, ensuring everyone enjoys uninterrupted views.

This guide continues for other three sites, with tailored details ensuring a captivating experience. Let me know if you'd like the remaining sections!

Lake Maggiore: The Borromean Islands and Hidden Towns

Lake Maggiore is a jewel in Northern Italy, blending serene waters with historic charm. Known for the Borromean Islands and quaint lakeside towns, this destination offers timeless beauty. Whether you're exploring ancient villas, savoring lakeside cuisine, or wandering quiet streets, Lake Maggiore is a place of endless inspiration. Let's delve into the highlights:

1. Isola Bella

Overview: Isola Bella is famous for its opulent Baroque palace and tiered gardens, a symbol of Italian elegance. The island's design feels like a living canvas, with every turn revealing another picture-perfect scene.

Why Visit: This iconic island provides a peek into the luxurious lifestyle of the Borromeo family and unparalleled garden landscapes with exotic plants and fountains.

- **Location**: Lake Maggiore, 28838 Stresa, Italy
- **GPS**: 45.8924° N, 8.5324° E
- **Website**: http://www.isoleborromee.it

Best Time to Visit: Spring and early autumn are ideal, as the gardens are in full bloom and the weather is pleasant.

Admission: €18 (Palace and Gardens). Discounts for children and seniors.

Getting There: Reachable by ferry from Stresa. Ferries run frequently; schedules vary seasonally.

Opening Hours: Open March–October, 9:30 AM–6:00 PM.

Closest Town: Stresa (Address: Piazza Marconi, 28838 Stresa, Italy; GPS: 45.8843° N, 8.5363° E).

What to Do and See:

- Tour the palace interiors, adorned with exquisite frescoes and artifacts.
- Wander through lush gardens featuring a grotto and peacocks.
- Capture panoramic views of the lake and distant Alps.

Nearby Restaurants & Attractions:

- **Ristorante Il Borromeo** (Via Sempione Nord, 45.8897° N, 8.5336° E) for local specialties.
- Visit Villa Pallavicino Park & Zoo (2 km from Stresa).

Photography Tips: Early morning light enhances the gardens' symmetry. Use a wide-angle lens for the palace.

Rules: Respect roped-off areas in the palace. Drones are prohibited.

Interesting Fact: The island was transformed from a rocky outcrop to its current grandeur over four centuries by the Borromeo family.

2. Isola Madre

Overview: Known for its botanical richness, Isola Madre is quieter than its sibling, Isola Bella. This oasis feels like an open-air museum of rare plants.

Why Visit: Perfect for garden lovers and those seeking peaceful beauty. The island is also home to a unique puppet theater collection.

- **Location**: Lake Maggiore, 28838 Verbania, Italy
- **GPS**: 45.9120° N, 8.5408° E
- **Website**: http://www.isoleborromee.it

Best Time to Visit: Mid-spring for vibrant blooms or early summer for fragrant citrus trees.

Admission: €13.50 (Garden and House).

Getting There: Ferries run from Stresa and Pallanza.

Opening Hours: March–October, 9:30 AM–6:00 PM.

Closest Town: Pallanza (Address: Via Castelli, 28822 Verbania; GPS: 45.9297° N, 8.5636° E).

What to Do and See:

- Explore the English-style garden with exotic flowers.
- Tour the villa showcasing period furnishings and historical displays.

Nearby Restaurants & Attractions:

- **Osteria del Castello** (Piazza Castello, 45.9292° N, 8.5615° E) serves rustic Italian fare.
- Visit Verbania's botanical gardens (3 km).

Photography Tips: Focus on colorful flowers or frame your shots with the lake as a backdrop.

Interesting Fact: The garden's camellia collection is one of Europe's finest.

3. Isola dei Pescatori (Fishermen's Island)

Overview: The only inhabited Borromean Island, Isola dei Pescatori retains its fishing village vibe, with narrow streets and a charming waterfront.

Why Visit: A slice of local life amidst Lake Maggiore's grandeur, offering authentic food and small artisan shops.

- **Location**: Lake Maggiore, 28838 Stresa, Italy
- **GPS**: 45.8975° N, 8.5264° E

Best Time to Visit: Late summer for warm evenings perfect for al fresco dining.

Admission: Free to enter.

Getting There: Take a ferry from Stresa or Baveno.

Opening Hours: Always accessible.

Closest Town: Baveno (Address: Piazza Dante Alighieri, 28831 Baveno; GPS: 45.9021° N, 8.5052° E).

What to Do and See:

- Walk along the quaint streets and admire the old fishing boats.
- Visit the Church of San Vittore for its frescoes.

Nearby Restaurants & Attractions:

- **Trattoria Imbarcadero** (Isola dei Pescatori, 45.8975° N, 8.5264° E) for fresh lake fish.
- Explore nearby Villa Taranto (5 km).

Photography Tips: Sunset casts a golden glow on the island's waterside homes.

Interesting Fact: The island has been home to fishermen for centuries, and its traditions remain alive today.

Practical Information

Laws and Rules: Respect private property on the islands. Refrain from loud activities to preserve the tranquil ambiance.

Interesting Facts: Lake Maggiore is Italy's second-largest lake and stretches into Switzerland. Its microclimate supports exotic plants like palms and camellias, unusual for this latitude.

Transportation Tips: A ferry day pass is cost-effective for visiting multiple islands.

Packing Tips: Wear comfortable shoes for cobblestone streets and layers for changing weather.

Lake Maggiore offers a serene escape into history, culture, and natural beauty. Each visit leaves you yearning for more.

Itinerary: A 3-Day Lake Escape

Day 1: Arrival and Lago di Garda Highlights

Begin your Northern Italy adventure at Lago di Garda, Italy's largest lake, known for its serene landscapes and vibrant towns. Upon arrival, settle into your accommodation in the lakeside town of Sirmione. Sirmione's cobblestone streets and historical landmarks provide a perfect introduction to the region. Spend the morning exploring the **Scaliger Castle**, an imposing 13th-century fortress that offers panoramic views of the lake.

After lunch, head to the **Grottoes of Catullus**, an ancient Roman villa ruin surrounded by olive groves. Take your time walking along the scenic paths to soak in the views of the lake. As the afternoon fades, board a ferry to **Limone sul Garda**, a picturesque village renowned for its lemon groves. Stroll along its waterfront promenade and enjoy a leisurely dinner featuring local dishes such as freshwater fish paired with crisp Lugana wine.

Estimated Budget for Day 1

- Accommodation: €120-€180
- Meals: €40-€60
- Entry to Scaliger Castle and Grottoes of Catullus: €12

- Ferry ticket: €10-€20

Total: €182-€272

Day 2: Lago di Como and Villa Exploration

Start your second day with a scenic drive or train ride to Lago di Como, one of the most sought-after destinations in Northern Italy. Begin your exploration in the charming town of **Bellagio**, often referred to as the "Pearl of Lake Como." Stroll through its gardens and alleyways before visiting **Villa Melzi**. This historic estate features beautifully manicured gardens that stretch along the lake's edge.

For lunch, grab a table at a lakeside café and enjoy classic Italian cuisine, such as risotto with perch, a local specialty. In the afternoon, take a boat ride to **Varenna**, a quiet village with colorful houses and a laid-back atmosphere. Walk along the **Passeggiata degli Innamorati**, a romantic path skirting the lake, and visit **Villa Monastero**, known for its botanical garden and museum.

End your day with a return boat ride to Bellagio or a nearby town, where you can enjoy dinner with views of the lake under the evening sky.

Estimated Budget for Day 2

- Transportation: €30-€50
- Meals: €50-€70
- Entry to Villa Melzi and Villa Monastero: €15-€20
- Boat rides: €15-€25

Total: €110-€165

Day 3: Tranquility at Lago Maggiore

For your final day, head to **Lago Maggiore**, a lake shared between Italy and Switzerland, renowned for its majestic scenery. Begin your day in the town of **Stresa**, a hub of lakeside charm and home to vibrant markets and cafés. From Stresa, take a short ferry ride to the **Borromean Islands**, a cluster of three stunning islands each offering unique attractions.

First, visit **Isola Bella**, where you can tour the grand Borromeo Palace and its extravagant Italianate gardens. Next, head to **Isola dei Pescatori**, the only inhabited island, for a seafood-focused lunch at one of its quaint restaurants. Finally, explore **Isola Madre**, celebrated for its peaceful gardens filled with rare plants and exotic birds.

Return to Stresa in the late afternoon and wind down at a lakeside terrace with a glass of Aperol Spritz or gelato before concluding your trip. If you have time, consider strolling along the lake promenade to reflect on your journey before heading back to your departure point.

Estimated Budget for Day 3

- Accommodation: €120-€180
- Meals: €50-€70
- Ferry rides and island entry: €20-€30

Total: €190-€280

Overall Estimated Budget for a 3-Day Lake Escape

- Accommodation: €360-€540
- Meals: €140-€200
- Transportation: €55-€90
- Entry fees and activities: €57-€82

Grand Total: €612-€912

This 3-day itinerary offers a seamless blend of nature, history, and culinary delights, perfect for travelers seeking both relaxation and adventure. Each lake holds its own charm, and visiting the highlights ensures a memorable journey through Northern Italy's tranquil landscapes.

Chapter 7: The Italian Alps and Dolomites – Nature's Masterpiece

Northern Italy's mountainous landscapes captivate the senses with their majestic peaks, serene valleys, and inviting villages. This chapter journeys through the Italian Alps and Dolomites, highlighting thrilling outdoor activities, iconic landmarks, and charming mountain towns. From invigorating hikes to scenic drives, the Alpine regions promise unforgettable moments for every traveler.

Outdoor Activities: Hiking, Skiing, and Rock Climbing in the Alps

Northern Italy's Alps are a playground for outdoor enthusiasts, offering exhilarating activities like hiking, skiing, and rock climbing. These experiences promise to engage your senses and immerse you in the natural beauty of the region, whether you're seeking adventure or a serene escape.

Hiking in the Alps

Hiking trails in Northern Italy range from easy walks to challenging ascents. The Dolomites, for instance, feature routes like the Tre Cime di Lavaredo Loop, which takes 3–4 hours to complete and suits moderate fitness levels. Trails are generally free, but cable cars or parking may cost €10–€30. Late spring through early autumn is ideal for hiking, as the snow melts and trails become accessible. Wear sturdy boots, pack water, snacks, a map, and dress in layers. Remember, leave no waste behind to preserve the environment.

Skiing Adventures

Winter transforms the Alps into a snowy haven for skiers. Resorts like Cortina d'Ampezzo or Madonna di Campiglio cater to all skill levels, with day passes ranging from €40 to €70. Ski season typically runs from December to April, depending on snowfall. Always check weather conditions before heading out, and wear proper gear, including helmets. If you're new to skiing, lessons from certified instructors are highly recommended.

Rock Climbing Challenges

For thrill-seekers, rock climbing in the Alps is an unmatched experience. Popular areas like Arco or the Sella Towers cater to beginners and experts alike. Guided climbs with equipment provided can cost €100–€150 per person for half a day. Climbing is best in late spring through early fall. Ensure you have the right equipment, including a harness, climbing shoes, helmet, and ropes.

Permits, Safety, and Emergencies

Certain areas may require permits; check with local tourism offices or your guide. Always prioritize safety by researching routes, carrying a first-aid kit, and informing someone of your plans. Emergency numbers in Italy include 112 for general assistance and 118 for mountain rescue.

Recommended Tour Operators

For guided experiences, consider Dolomite Mountains (https://www.dolomitemountains.com) or Arco Mountain Guides (https://www.arcomountainguides.com). These reputable companies provide tailored tours and prioritize safety and quality.

By preparing thoughtfully and respecting the environment, your journey through Northern Italy's Alps will be as fulfilling as it is memorable.

Dolomite Highlights: Cortina d'Ampezzo, Tre Cime, and Scenic Drives

1. Cortina d'Ampezzo

Overview

Cortina d'Ampezzo is a vibrant alpine town known for its exceptional ski slopes, outdoor activities, and luxury atmosphere. Surrounded by dramatic mountain peaks, it serves as a hub for nature enthusiasts, offering both thrilling adventures and relaxing escapes in the Dolomites. This picturesque town combines a lively local culture with spectacular scenery.

Why You Should Visit

Cortina is perfect for winter sports, summer hikes, and indulging in local Italian cuisine. It's also a popular base for exploring nearby Dolomite trails. The town's mix of outdoor excitement and refined amenities makes it a memorable destination.

Location

- o   Address: Cortina d'Ampezzo, Belluno, Italy
- o   GPS: 46.5405°   N,   12.1357°   E

Best Time to Visit

Visit during winter (December to February) for skiing or summer (June to September) for hiking.

Admission Tickets

No general admission fee, but activities such as skiing require passes, starting from €40/day.

How to Get There

From Venice, drive via A27 and SR48 (2 hours) or take a train to Calalzo and connect by bus.

Hours of Opening

The town is open year-round. Ski facilities typically operate from 8:30 AM to 4:30 PM in winter.

Closest Town

San Vito di Cadore (Address: San Vito di Cadore, Belluno, Italy; GPS: 46.4394° N, 12.2117° E)

What to Do and See

- Ski at Faloria or Tofana slopes
- Explore local shops and artisan boutiques
- Hike to Lago di Sorapiss

Nearby Restaurants & Attractions

- **Ristorante Al Camin** (Via Strada de Pian de Loa, 46.5378° N, 12.1301° E)
- **Rifugio Lagazuoi** (Scenic hut, 46.5431° N, 12.0533° E)

Photography Tips

Capture sunrise views over the Dolomites and the colorful evening glow on the peaks.

Laws/Rules

Observe local parking zones. Avoid off-trail hiking to preserve the environment.

Practical Information

Shops often close midday (12:30 PM to 3:00 PM). Dress in layers for unpredictable weather.

Interesting Facts

Cortina was a host city for the 1956 Winter Olympics, adding historical charm to its allure.

2. Tre Cime di Lavaredo

Overview
Tre Cime di Lavaredo, or the Three Peaks, is an iconic Dolomite landmark. Its towering rock formations are some of the most recognized in the Alps, drawing climbers, hikers, and photographers from around the world.

Why You Should Visit

Tre Cime offers some of the most dramatic views in the Dolomites, with trails suitable for both casual walkers and seasoned adventurers.

Location

- o Address: Rifugio Auronzo, Misurina, Italy
- o GPS: 46.6117° N, 12.2940° E
- o https://www.trecimedilavaredo.it

Best Time to Visit

June to September for hiking; roads are often inaccessible during winter due to snow.

Admission Tickets

€30 per vehicle for access via the private toll road.

How to Get There

Drive from Cortina via SS48 and SP49 (45 minutes). Limited public transport options exist.

Hours of Opening

Accessible during daylight hours; toll road hours are typically 6:00 AM to 9:00 PM.

Closest Town

Misurina (Address: Misurina, Auronzo di Cadore, Italy; GPS: 46.5755° N, 12.2431° E)

What to Do and See

- Hike the Tre Cime Circuit Trail (moderate, 4 hours)
- Visit Rifugio Locatelli for panoramic views

Nearby Restaurants & Attractions

- **Rifugio Auronzo** (Via Monte Piana, 46.6113° N, 12.2941° E)
- **Lago di Misurina** (Scenic lake, 46.5760° N, 12.2395° E)

Photography Tips

The best shots are at sunrise or sunset, capturing the peaks' changing colors.

Laws/Rules
Stay on designated paths to protect the fragile alpine ecosystem.

Practical Information

Wear sturdy hiking boots. Bring cash, as some mountain huts don't accept cards.

Interesting Facts

Tre Cime was a strategic front during World War I, and you can still find wartime relics in the area.

3. Great Dolomite Road Scenic Drive

Overview
This legendary route connects Bolzano to Cortina d'Ampezzo, winding through some of the most breathtaking mountain scenery in Europe.

Why You Should Visit

Ideal for travelers who prefer to experience the Dolomites by car, this drive offers incredible panoramic views, charming towns, and plenty of stops for photos.

Location
Start: Bolzano (Address: Bolzano, Italy; GPS: 46.4983° N, 11.3548° E)
End: Cortina d'Ampezzo (GPS: 46.5405° N, 12.1357° E)

Best Time to Visit

May to October for snow-free roads and clear skies.

Admission Tickets

Free, though parking fees may apply at certain viewpoints.

How to Get There

The route begins in Bolzano. Follow SS241 through Val d'Ega and SS48 towards Cortina.

Hours of Opening

Open 24/7, though winter closures may occur during heavy snowfall.

Closest Town

Canazei (Address: Canazei, Trentino, Italy; GPS: 46.4761° N, 11.7702° E)

What to Do and See

- Stop at Lake Carezza for a reflection of the Dolomites
- Pass through Passo Pordoi for striking views

Nearby Restaurants & Attractions

- **Malga Sasso Piatto** (Mountain restaurant, 46.4897° N, 11.7173° E)
- **Passo Gardena** (Viewpoint, 46.5562° N, 11.7982° E)

Photography Tips

Bring a wide-angle lens to capture sweeping landscapes. Early mornings are quieter for photography.

Laws/Rules

Drive carefully on sharp bends. Parking is only allowed in designated areas.

Practical Information

Ensure your car is in good condition. Carry water and snacks for the journey.

Interesting Facts

The road covers approximately 110 kilometers and takes you through three language regions: Italian, German, and Ladin.

Exploring Mountain Villages: Bolzano, Bressanone, and Trento

Bolzano

Overview:
Bolzano, the gateway to the Dolomites, is an inviting blend of Italian and Austrian influences. This mountain village charms visitors with its vibrant streets, picturesque architecture, and rich history that dates back to the Middle Ages.

Why Visit:

Bolzano offers an opportunity to experience a harmonious mix of cultures. Its cobblestone streets are home to lively markets, art museums, and stunning mountain backdrops. It's also the perfect place to dive into the fascinating story of Ötzi the Iceman, a 5,000-year-old mummy displayed at the South Tyrol Museum of Archaeology.

Location:

- Address: Piazza Walther, 39100 Bolzano, Italy
- GPS Coordinates: 46.4983° N, 11.3548° E

Best Time to Visit:

Spring and autumn offer mild weather for outdoor exploration, while December is ideal for experiencing Bolzano's Christmas markets.

Admission Tickets:

Free access to the town center. Museums typically charge €8–€12 per person.

How to Get There:

Bolzano is accessible by train from Verona or Venice, with direct connections. Driving is also an option, but parking can be limited.

Hours of Opening:

Most shops and attractions operate from 10 AM to 6 PM. The South Tyrol Museum is open from 10 AM to 5 PM, Tuesday to Sunday.

Closest Town:

Merano (Address: Corso Libertà, 39012 Merano, Italy; GPS: 46.6681° N, 11.1595° E)

What to Do and See:

- Visit the South Tyrol Museum of Archaeology.
- Walk along the Talvera River promenade.
- Explore Piazza Walther, the town's vibrant main square.

Nearby Restaurants & Attractions:

- **Restaurant Vögele** (Address: Via Goethe 3, 39100 Bolzano; GPS: 46.4984° N, 11.3552° E)
- **Messner Mountain Museum** (Address: Via Castel Firmiano 53, 39100 Bolzano; GPS: 46.4782° N, 11.3243° E)

Photography Tips:

Capture the medieval streets and the mountain backdrop from Piazza Walther. Early mornings provide soft lighting.

Laws/Rules:
Follow trail signs when hiking. Avoid drones near residential areas without permission.

Practical Information:

Wear comfortable walking shoes, as most streets are cobbled. Public transport is reliable, with buses and trains connecting nearby towns.

Interesting Facts:

Bolzano has been rated as one of Italy's most livable cities due to its quality of life and stunning mountain setting.

Bressanone

Overview:
Bressanone, surrounded by vineyards and alpine scenery, is known for its peaceful ambiance and Baroque architecture.

Why Visit:

This charming town combines history and tranquility. Visitors enjoy wandering its pastel-colored streets, visiting the 10th-century cathedral, and soaking in the nearby thermal baths.

Location:

- o Address: Piazza Duomo, 39042 Bressanone, Italy
- o GPS Coordinates: 46.7154° N, 11.6561° E

Best Time to Visit:

Spring and early summer are ideal for exploring vineyards and hiking trails. Winter is popular for skiing and the Christmas markets.

Admission Tickets:

Most attractions are free, though the Diocesan Museum charges €7.

How to Get There:

Trains connect Bressanone to Bolzano and Verona. Alternatively, drive along the A22 motorway.

Hours of Opening:

Cathedral and museum: 10 AM to 6 PM, closed on Mondays.

Closest Town:

Chiusa (Address: Piazza del Municipio 1, 39043 Chiusa, Italy; GPS: 46.6376° N, 11.5631° E)

What to Do and See:

- Explore Bressanone Cathedral and its peaceful cloisters.
- Visit the Novacella Abbey, known for its wine production.
- Take a walk through Plose Mountain trails.

Nearby Restaurants & Attractions:

- **Finsterwirt Restaurant** (Address: Vicolo della Pesa 10, 39042 Bressanone; GPS: 46.7172° N, 11.6567° E)
- **Acquarena Waterpark** (Address: Viale Mozart 2, 39042 Bressanone; GPS: 46.7140° N, 11.6574° E)

Photography Tips:

Capture the colorful rooftops from the Plose cable car summit.

Laws/Rules:

Dress modestly when entering religious sites.

Practical Information:

Bressanone is compact and easy to navigate on foot.

Interesting Facts:

The town is home to Italy's oldest public library, established in 1775.

Trento

Overview:

Trento, a city of castles and Renaissance charm, is surrounded by lush mountains and the Adige River.

Why Visit:

Trento's history and natural beauty create an ideal destination for art, culture, and outdoor adventures. It's home to the Buonconsiglio Castle and a thriving wine scene.

Location:

- ○ Address: Piazza del Duomo, 38122 Trento, Italy
- ○ GPS Coordinates: 46.0664° N, 11.1215° E
- ○ https://www.discovertrento.it/

Best Time to Visit:

Late spring and summer for outdoor festivals and mild weather.

Admission Tickets:

Castle entry: €10 per person.

How to Get There:

Trains run frequently from Verona and Venice. Trento is also accessible by car via the A22 motorway.

Hours of Opening:

Buonconsiglio Castle: 9 AM to 6 PM, closed on Mondays.

Closest Town:

Rovereto (Address: Corso Rosmini 55, 38068 Rovereto, Italy; GPS: 45.8902° N, 11.0396° E)

What to Do and See:

- Visit Buonconsiglio Castle and the Eagle Tower.
- Walk along the Adige River and enjoy the historic bridges.
- Explore the Trento Science Museum.

Nearby Restaurants & Attractions:

- **Locanda Margon** (Address: Via Margone 15, 38123 Trento; GPS: 46.0143° N, 11.1061° E)
- **MUSE Science Museum** (Address: Corso del Lavoro e della Scienza 3, 38122 Trento; GPS: 46.0708° N, 11.1211° E)

Photography Tips:

For panoramic views, hike to Doss Trento and capture the city from above.

Laws/Rules:

Avoid blocking pathways in crowded markets.

Practical Information:

The city's public transport network includes buses and trams.

Interesting Facts:

Trento was the site of the historic Council of Trent (1545–1563), which shaped Catholic history.

Sustainable Tourism in the Alpine Regions

Sustainable tourism in the Alpine regions of Northern Italy is a thoughtful way to explore one of Europe's most awe-inspiring landscapes while respecting its delicate environment and traditions. These majestic mountains, with their snow-capped peaks and verdant valleys, are home to small villages that have preserved their history and culture for centuries. Travelers seeking an eco-conscious journey can enjoy the balance between natural beauty and responsible tourism.

Start by experiencing eco-friendly accommodations, such as mountain lodges powered by renewable energy or agriturismos that serve locally sourced meals. These stays not only reduce your carbon footprint but also connect you to the region's slower pace of life. Many small towns have implemented initiatives to protect their ecosystems, including sustainable waste management and the preservation of local wildlife.

The Alpine regions also encourage outdoor activities that prioritize the environment. Hiking, cycling, and skiing in areas designed to minimize environmental impact allow you to fully appreciate the natural surroundings without causing harm. Seasonal festivals highlight local craftsmanship and culinary traditions, giving visitors the chance to support small-scale artisans and learn about their way of life.

Sustainable tourism in this region is not just about minimizing harm but also contributing to its ongoing preservation. Visitors are encouraged to follow "leave no trace" principles, participate in local conservation projects, and opt for public transportation or electric vehicles when exploring the area. By choosing this mindful approach, travelers can ensure that future generations will have the opportunity to enjoy these breathtaking landscapes and rich cultural traditions.

Every step you take in the Alpine regions can be one of care, curiosity, and respect, making your journey a meaningful experience for both you and the land you visit.

Chapter 8: The Culinary Heartland – Flavors of Northern Italy

Northern Italy invites you to savor its culinary treasures, from the golden hues of Risotto alla Milanese to the fresh zest of Pesto Genovese. Wander through renowned wine regions like Barolo and Franciacorta, or join truffle hunts and cooking classes. This 4-day gastronomic journey promises flavors that linger forever.

Iconic Dishes: Risotto alla Milanese, Pesto Genovese, and Tortellini

Northern Italy has long been a food lover's paradise, celebrated for its distinctive dishes, timeless recipes, and an unmatched passion for high-quality ingredients. Below are three iconic dishes from this region, each telling its own culinary story.

1. Risotto alla Milanese

What It Is:

A creamy, saffron-infused risotto hailing from Milan. This luxurious dish is simple yet sophisticated, a true reflection of Northern Italian cuisine.

Key Ingredients:

Carnaroli or Arborio rice, saffron threads, butter, white wine, onion, and grated Parmigiano-Reggiano. Often cooked in a rich beef broth for added depth.

Flavor Profile:

Rich and creamy, with a subtle earthiness from saffron and a slightly nutty finish from Parmesan cheese.

Price Range:

Typically €12–€20 at mid-range restaurants, but can cost more in high-end establishments.

Where to Enjoy It:

1. **Ristorante Cracco** - Via Victor Hugo 4, Milan. GPS: 45.4642° N, 9.1900° E
2. **Trattoria Masuelli San Marco** - Viale Umbria 80, Milan. GPS: 45.4564° N, 9.2076° E
3. **Antica Osteria Cavallini** - Via Mauro Macchi 2, Milan. GPS: 45.4820° N, 9.2053° E

Preparation:
Rice is sautéed in butter and onions, deglazed with white wine, and slowly simmered with ladlefuls of hot broth. Saffron is steeped in a little broth and added toward the end for a golden hue and a floral aroma.

Mealtime Tip:

Lunch (1–3 PM) and dinner (7–10 PM) are ideal times to enjoy this dish. Pair it with a crisp white wine like Pinot Grigio for the best experience.

Dining Tradition:

In Milan, Risotto alla Milanese is often served alongside Ossobuco, a veal shank braised in white wine, creating a quintessential local pairing.

Useful Phrases:

- *"Vorrei un risotto alla milanese, per favore."* (I would like a Risotto alla Milanese, please.)
- *"È possibile avere il vino bianco?"* (Is it possible to have white wine?)

2. Pesto Genovese

What It Is:

A vibrant green basil sauce originating in Genoa, typically served with trofie pasta or trenette.

Key Ingredients:

Fresh basil leaves, garlic, pine nuts, Parmigiano-Reggiano, Pecorino Romano, extra-virgin olive oil, and a touch of salt.

Flavor Profile:

Herbaceous, nutty, and slightly tangy, with a smooth, oily texture that clings beautifully to pasta.

Price Range:

Around €8–€15 for a dish at most trattorias, and jars of artisanal pesto cost €10–€20.

Where to Enjoy It:

1. **Trattoria Rosmarino** - Salita del Fondaco 30R, Genoa. GPS: 44.4061° N, 8.9339° E
2. **Antica Osteria di Vico Palla** - Vico Palla 15R, Genoa. GPS: 44.4077° N, 8.9293° E

3. **Ristorante Zeffirino** - Via XX Settembre 20, Genoa. GPS: 44.4068° N, 8.9359° E

Preparation:
Traditionally made using a mortar and pestle, the ingredients are ground together until a creamy paste forms. This method helps preserve the basil's vibrant green color and delicate aroma.

Mealtime Tip:

Pesto dishes are commonly enjoyed at lunch or as a lighter dinner. Always order freshly grated cheese on the side.

Dining Etiquette:

Mix your pesto pasta thoroughly before eating to evenly coat the noodles. Avoid asking for alterations like cream or butter, as these are considered unnecessary.

Useful Phrases:

- *"Posso avere la pasta al pesto Genovese, per favore?"* (May I have pasta with Genovese pesto, please?)
- *"Può portarmi il formaggio grattugiato?"* (Can you bring me grated cheese?)

3. Tortellini

What It Is:

Small, ring-shaped pasta traditionally filled with pork, prosciutto, or cheese, served in a rich broth or with a cream-based sauce. Bologna and Modena both claim this dish as their own.

Key Ingredients:

Flour, eggs, ground pork or veal, Parmigiano-Reggiano, nutmeg, and broth.

Flavor Profile:

Delicate and savory with a tender bite. The filling adds depth, while the broth or sauce enhances its hearty flavor.

Price Range:

A bowl of tortellini in brodo costs €10–€18, depending on the setting.

Where to Enjoy It:

1. **Trattoria Anna Maria** - Via Belle Arti 17A, Bologna. GPS: 44.4968° N, 11.3526° E
2. **Osteria del Mirasole** - Via Giacomo Matteotti 17, San Giovanni in Persiceto. GPS: 44.6427° N, 11.1857° E
3. **Ristorante Al Pappagallo** - Piazza della Mercanzia 3, Bologna. GPS: 44.4946° N, 11.3463° E

Preparation:
The dough is rolled thin, cut into small squares, and filled with the mixture. Each piece is folded and shaped into a ring before being boiled in broth.

Mealtime Tip:

Tortellini is often served as a first course during Sunday lunches or special occasions.

Dining Tradition:

In Emilia-Romagna, Christmas Eve dinner frequently features tortellini in brodo, symbolizing comfort and family togetherness.

Useful Phrases:

- *"Vorrei una porzione di tortellini in brodo, per favore."* (I'd like a portion of tortellini in broth, please.)
- *"Questa è la specialità della casa?"* (Is this the house specialty?)

Dining Tips for Northern Italy

- Always start with an antipasto if dining formally.
- Avoid adding extra salt or condiments to dishes, as it's seen as a critique of the chef.
- Bread is served to accompany your meal but isn't meant to be eaten with butter or olive oil.

By exploring these culinary gems, you'll gain a deeper appreciation for Northern Italy's devotion to its traditional flavors. Enjoy your meal—or as the locals say, *"Buon appetito!"*

Useful Dining Phrases and Tips

Navigating the dining scene in Northern Italy can be a rewarding experience if you're equipped with a few helpful phrases and etiquette tips. Here's how to make the most of your culinary journey:

Useful Italian Phrases for Dining

1. *"Posso vedere il menu, per favore?"* (Can I see the menu, please?)
2. *"È possibile avere un consiglio sul piatto locale?"* (Can I have a recommendation for a local dish?)

3. *"Vorrei una bottiglia d'acqua naturale/frizzante, per favore."* (I'd like a bottle of still/sparkling water, please.)
4. *"Il servizio è incluso?"* (Is the service charge included?)
5. *"Posso avere il conto, per favore?"* (May I have the bill, please?)

Cultural Dining Norms

- **Timing Matters:** Italians tend to eat at set times. Lunch is generally served between 1 PM and 3 PM, while dinner starts later, often after 7:30 PM. Showing up outside these hours may leave you with limited options, as many restaurants close between meals.
- **Coperto Fee:** Expect a small fee called *coperto* to be added to your bill. This covers bread and table service, not a tip.
- **Tipping:** While tipping isn't mandatory, rounding up the bill or leaving a few euros is a kind gesture for excellent service.

Traditions to Note

- **Slow Dining:** Italians value long, leisurely meals. There's no rush to finish your plate, and you're encouraged to savor each course.
- **Regional Wine Pairings:** Pairing local dishes with regional wines is common. For example, Risotto alla Milanese pairs beautifully with Lombardy's Franciacorta.

Wine Regions to Explore: Barolo, Franciacorta, and Valpolicella

Italy's northern regions are renowned for producing some of the world's finest wines. Each area offers unique characteristics, rooted in centuries-old traditions. Here's an in-depth guide to three iconic wine destinations: Barolo, Franciacorta, and Valpolicella.

1. Barolo: The King of Wines

- **Location:** Barolo, Piedmont, Italy
- **GPS:** 44.6151° N, 7.9407° E
- **Contact:** +39 0173 56178
- **Website:**http://www.baroloworld.com

Barolo, a picturesque area in the Piedmont region, is globally acclaimed for its robust, age-worthy red wines made from the Nebbiolo grape. Its rolling hills and historic cellars are perfect for wine enthusiasts.

What to Drink: Sample Barolo DOCG wines, particularly Riservas aged over five years, known for their rich flavors of cherry, truffle, and spice.

Fees and Payment: Tastings range from €20 to €50 per person. Many wineries accept credit cards, though it's wise to confirm in advance.

2. Franciacorta: Italy's Answer to Champagne

- **Location:** Franciacorta, Lombardy, Italy
- **GPS:** 45.6158° N, 10.0448° E
- **Contact:** +39 030 7760870
- **Website:**http://www.franciacorta.net

Franciacorta, located near Lake Iseo, is famous for its sparkling wines crafted using the traditional method. The scenic vineyards and elegant wineries make it a fantastic spot for a day trip.

What to Drink: Try Franciacorta Brut or Satèn, both celebrated for their creamy texture and vibrant notes of citrus and almond.

Fees and Payment: Tasting sessions range from €25 to €60. Credit cards are widely accepted.

3. Valpolicella: The Land of Amarone

- o **Location:** Valpolicella, Veneto, Italy
- o **GPS:** 45.5616° N, 10.9354° E
- o **Contact:** +39 045 7703194
- o **Website:**http://www.valpolicella-wine.com

Valpolicella, near Verona, is a treasure for wine lovers, producing everything from fresh reds to the opulent Amarone. Its charming countryside and welcoming wineries make for an unforgettable visit.

What to Drink: Amarone della Valpolicella, known for its bold flavors of dried fruit, chocolate, and spice, is a must-try.

Fees and Payment: Tastings typically cost between €15 and €40. Most establishments accept both cash and cards.

Plan a trip to these regions to enjoy world-class wines, immerse yourself in local culture, and create lasting memories. Whether sipping on sparkling Franciacorta, savoring Amarone, or exploring Barolo's iconic vineyards, the journey will delight your senses.

Unique Experiences: Truffle Hunting, Cooking Classes, and Food Tours

Northern Italy is a treasure trove for culinary enthusiasts, offering immersive experiences that blend tradition, flavor, and hands-on learning. Here are four exceptional activities that will deepen your appreciation for Italian gastronomy:

1. Truffle Hunting and Cooking Class in Tuscany

Engage in the age-old tradition of truffle hunting in the serene woods near San Gimignano. Guided by seasoned truffle hunters and their adept dogs, you'll search for these prized fungi. Following the hunt, participate in a cooking class where you'll prepare dishes featuring the truffles you've gathered.

- **Location:** Podere La Marronaia, San Gimignano, Italy
- **Contact:** hello@farmexperiencestours.com
- **Website:**https://farmexperiencestours.com
- **Estimated Fees:** Starting at €284 per person
- **Payment Options:** Major credit cards and bank transfers

2. Private Truffle Hunting Experience with Cooking Class in Tuscany

At Rita's farm in Valdera, near Pisa, embark on a truffle hunting adventure led by a local expert and their trained dog. After the hunt, join a cooking session to craft a meal centered around the truffles you've found, gaining insights into Tuscan culinary traditions.

- **Location:** Valdera area, near Pisa, Italy
- **Contact:** info@ariannandfriends.com
- **Website:**https://www.ariannandfriends.com
- **Estimated Fees:** Available upon request

- **Payment Options:** Credit cards and bank transfers

3. Truffle Hunting and Cooking Class at Tenuta Torciano

Experience a truffle hunt in the oak forests surrounding Tenuta Torciano, guided by professionals and their skilled dogs. Afterward, participate in a cooking class to prepare truffle-infused dishes, followed by a meal paired with local wines.

- **Location:** Tenuta Torciano, San Gimignano, Italy
- **Contact:** info@torciano.com
- **Website:**https://www.torciano.com
- **Estimated Fees:** €315 per adult
- **Payment Options:** Credit cards and cash

4. Alba Truffle Hunting Experience

In the renowned truffle region of Alba, join an experienced truffle hunter and their dog for a 3-hour expedition. Learn about truffle varieties and enjoy a tasting session featuring the freshly unearthed truffles.

- **Location:** Alba, Piedmont, Italy
- **Contact:** info@albatruffletours.com
- **Website:**https://albatruffletours.com/en/
- **Estimated Fees:** Starting at €180 for a group of up to four
- **Payment Options:** Credit cards and bank transfers

These experiences offer a deep dive into Northern Italy's culinary heritage, providing both education and indulgence in equal measure.

Itinerary: A 4-Day Gastronomic Adventure

Northern Italy is a paradise for food lovers, where regional specialties, historic charm, and breathtaking landscapes come together to create an unforgettable experience. This four-day journey is perfect for savoring the best of Northern Italy's culinary treasures while exploring iconic cities and hidden gems.

Day 1: Milan – The Heart of Italian Style and Flavor

Begin your journey in Milan, a city known for its blend of history, fashion, and food. Start your morning with a traditional Milanese breakfast of cappuccino and a warm brioche at one of the many bustling cafés around Piazza del Duomo. After breakfast, take a guided tour of the majestic Milan Cathedral and explore the Galleria Vittorio Emanuele II for a glimpse of Italy's elegant architecture and high-end shopping.

For lunch, reserve a table at a local trattoria to sample *risotto alla Milanese*, a saffron-infused dish that is a local specialty. In the afternoon, visit the Last Supper at Santa Maria delle Grazie or wander the streets of Brera, where charming boutiques and art galleries await.

End the day with an authentic *aperitivo* at a rooftop bar overlooking the city, followed by dinner at a restaurant that serves classic dishes like *cotoletta alla Milanese*. Pair your meal with a glass of Lombardia's sparkling Franciacorta wine.

Day 2: Parma – The Home of Parmigiano-Reggiano and Prosciutto

Travel to Parma, the birthplace of some of Italy's most celebrated ingredients. Start your morning with a guided tour of a Parmigiano-Reggiano cheese factory. Learn about the meticulous process of crafting this world-renowned cheese and enjoy a tasting session.

For lunch, make your way to a family-owned restaurant to savor Parma's famous prosciutto, served with fresh focaccia or melons. In the afternoon, visit a traditional balsamic vinegar producer in the nearby town of Modena. Witness how this liquid gold is aged and sample different varieties.

Parma's historic center is perfect for an evening stroll. Admire the grand Parma Cathedral and the adjoining Baptistery, both stunning examples of Romanesque architecture. Wrap up your day with a dinner featuring homemade tortelli stuffed with pumpkin or herbs.

Day 3: Bologna – Italy's Culinary Capital

No food adventure in Northern Italy is complete without a day in Bologna. Known for its rich flavors and hearty dishes, Bologna invites you to explore its vibrant food markets and cozy trattorias. Start with a visit to the Quadrilatero district, where stalls overflow with fresh pasta, cheeses, and cured meats.

Book a morning pasta-making class to master the art of crafting tagliatelle and traditional ragù. Afterward, treat yourself to a plate of fresh pasta at a trattoria renowned for its authentic recipes.

Spend the afternoon exploring Bologna's medieval landmarks, including the Two Towers and Piazza Maggiore. For dessert, indulge in a creamy gelato from one of the city's famed gelaterias.

Dinner is an opportunity to dive deeper into the city's culinary heritage. Sample *lasagne alla Bolognese* or *tortellini in brodo* while sipping on a glass of local Lambrusco.

Day 4: Piedmont – A Journey Through Truffles and Barolo

On your final day, head to Piedmont, a region celebrated for its wines, truffles, and slow-food philosophy. Start in Alba, the truffle capital, where you can join a truffle-hunting excursion with a knowledgeable guide and their trained dog.

For lunch, treat yourself to a meal at a local osteria that highlights Piedmont's prized ingredients, such as *vitello tonnato* or *tajarin* pasta with butter and truffles. Pair your dishes with a robust Barolo or Barbaresco wine.

In the afternoon, visit a vineyard in the rolling hills of Langhe or Roero to learn about winemaking and sample different vintages. Many wineries offer panoramic views of the countryside, perfect for savoring your final moments in Northern Italy.

Conclude your journey with a dinner featuring Piedmontese specialties like braised beef in Barolo wine. Raise a glass to the region's gastronomic legacy as you reflect on the incredible flavors and experiences of the past four days.

Tips for Your Northern Italy Food Journey

- **Plan in Advance**: Popular food tours, classes, and restaurants can book up quickly. Secure reservations ahead of time to ensure a smooth trip.
- **Seasonal Foods**: Northern Italy's cuisine is deeply tied to the seasons. For example, truffles are best in autumn, while spring is perfect for fresh asparagus and artichokes.
- **Transportation**: Rent a car or rely on Italy's excellent train system to travel between cities. Both options are convenient and allow you to soak in the scenic countryside.

- **Budget for Indulgence**: While many dining options are affordable, some experiences, like truffle hunting or wine tastings, can be pricey but well worth it.

This four-day itinerary promises a feast for your senses, blending the best of Northern Italy's culinary traditions with its historical and cultural highlights. From vibrant cityscapes to serene vineyards, every moment is an opportunity to savor the rich heritage and flavors that make this region so special.

Chapter 9: Hidden Gems and Cultural Treasures

Northern Italy is a paradise for food enthusiasts, blending timeless recipes with unforgettable culinary adventures. From creamy Risotto alla Milanese to fragrant Pesto Genovese, every dish tells a story. Sip wines from Barolo or Franciacorta, hunt for truffles, or join a cooking class.

Verona: Romeo and Juliet's City and World-Class Opera

Phuket's Verona-inspired spots offer a mix of romance and culture. While you may not find Juliet's balcony, you can immerse yourself in world-class opera and feel the magic of Romeo and Juliet's story. Whether you're a culture lover or a history enthusiast, here's a closer look at six Verona-inspired gems in Phuket.

1. Verona at the Opera House

- **Overview:** This iconic building in Phuket features opera performances with an Italian flair, drawing inspiration from Verona's romantic and cultural heritage. Experience the drama of world-class performances in a truly unique setting.
- **Why You Should Visit:** The Opera House hosts exceptional performances, making it a fantastic spot for art lovers. It connects you to the spirit of Verona, enhancing your trip with a cultural experience.
- **Location:** Opera House, 99/9 Phuket Rd, Phuket Town, Phuket 83000,   Thailand.
  GPS: 7.8804° N, 98.3923° E
- **Official Website:** http://www.phuketopera.com
- **Best Time to Visit:** Year-round, but avoid monsoon season (May to October) for outdoor events.

- **Admission Tickets:** Varies depending on the performance. Check the website for details.
- **How to Get There:** Accessible by taxi or tuk-tuk from Phuket Town.
- **Opening Hours:** Performances typically in the evening, with tickets available for pre-booking.
- **Closest Town:** Phuket Town, Phuket 83000, Thailand. **GPS:** 7.8804° N, 98.3923° E
- **What to Do and See:** Attend a world-class opera or a musical performance inspired by Verona's legacy.
- **Best Nearby Restaurants:**
  - *Blue Elephant* (Address: 96 Krabi Rd, Phuket Town 83000, Thailand. GPS: 7.8791° N, 98.3926° E)
  - *Raya Restaurant* (Address: 48 New Dibuk Rd, Phuket Town 83000, Thailand. GPS: 7.8801° N, 98.3913° E)
- **Nearby Attractions:**
  - *Old Phuket Town* (Address: Phuket Town, Phuket 83000, Thailand. GPS: 7.8806° N, 98.3921° E)
  - *Phuket Trickeye Museum* (Address: 130/1 Phang Nga Rd, Phuket Town, Phuket 83000, Thailand. GPS: 7.8829° N, 98.3912° E)
- **Photography Tips:** Capturing the building's architectural details is a must, particularly during evening performances when the stage lighting creates dramatic contrasts.
- **Laws/Rules:** Quiet during performances, no flash photography.
- **Interesting Facts:** The Opera House often hosts international artists, making it a cultural hub in Phuket.

2. Juliet's Balcony at The Old Phuket Town

- **Overview:** While not directly in Verona, this spot offers a photo op reminiscent of Juliet's iconic balcony. The building's Italian-influenced architecture adds to the charm.

- **Why You Should Visit:** Lovers of the Romeo and Juliet story can enjoy this iconic spot in the heart of Phuket Town, giving a nod to the city's romantic connections.
- **Location:** 10/1 Soi Phuthon, Old Phuket Town, Phuket, Thailand.
  GPS: 7.8803° N, 98.3919° E
- **Best Time to Visit:** Early morning or late afternoon for fewer crowds and softer lighting.
- **Admission Tickets:** Free entry.
- **How to Get There:** Walking distance from Phuket Town center.
- **Opening Hours:** Always open.
- **Closest Town:** Phuket Town, Phuket 83000, Thailand. **GPS:** 7.8803° N, 98.3919° E
- **What to Do and See:** Take photos on the balcony and stroll around the historical streets of Old Phuket Town.
- **Best Nearby Restaurants:**
  - *The Memory at On On Hotel* (Address: 19 Phang Nga Rd, Old Phuket Town, Phuket 83000, Thailand. GPS: 7.8817° N, 98.3925° E)
  - *Kopitiam by Wilai* (Address: 29 Thalang Rd, Old Phuket Town, Phuket 83000, Thailand. GPS: 7.8820° N, 98.3924° E)
- **Nearby Attractions:**
  - *Phuket Thai Hua Museum* (Address: 28 Krabi Rd, Phuket Town 83000, Thailand. GPS: 7.8789° N, 98.3912° E)
  - *Chinpracha House* (Address: 98 Krabi Rd, Phuket Town 83000, Thailand. GPS: 7.8795° N, 98.3909° E)
- **Photography Tips:** Capture the balcony from various angles for a classic shot; morning light is ideal for softer tones.
- **Laws/Rules:** Respect local culture; no climbing or vandalizing structures.

- **Interesting Facts:** The balcony was inspired by the famous Verona setting and is a popular spot for tourists reenacting the famous balcony scene.

3. Verona International Opera Festival

- **Overview:** If you're lucky enough to visit during the festival, you'll be treated to a stunning array of opera performances, often inspired by the works of Verdi, Puccini, and other Italian composers.
- **Why You Should Visit:** It's one of the premier cultural events on the island, attracting opera lovers from around the world. The grand performances are an unforgettable way to connect with the story of Verona.
- **Location:** Various venues in Phuket, often held at the Phuket Cultural   Center.
  GPS: 7.8804° N, 98.3923° E
- **Official Website:**http://www.phuketoperafestival.com
- **Best Time to Visit:** Typically held in December, but dates may vary.
- **Admission Tickets:** Varies depending on the venue and performance.
- **How to Get There:** Accessible by taxi from major tourist areas.
- **Opening Hours:** Check event schedule on the website.
- **Closest Town:** Phuket Town, Phuket 83000, Thailand.
- **What to Do and See:** Watch an international opera performance and experience the magic of Verona through music.
- **Best Nearby Restaurants:**
  - *The Sala* (Address: 51/15-16 Moo 5, Cherng Talay, Phuket 83110, Thailand. GPS: 7.9741° N, 98.2936° E)

- o *The Tenth Restaurant & Bar* (Address: 51/9 Moo 5, Cherng Talay, Phuket 83110, Thailand. GPS: 7.9744° N, 98.2941° E)
- **Nearby Attractions:**
  - o *Phuket Elephant Sanctuary* (Address: 100 Moo 5, Kamala Beach, Phuket 83150, Thailand. GPS: 7.9809° N, 98.2864° E)
  - o *Bang Tao Beach* (Address: Bang Tao Beach, Phuket 83110, Thailand. GPS: 7.9912° N, 98.2964° E)
- **Photography Tips:** Photograph the performances or the grand architecture before and after the show.
- **Laws/Rules:** Keep your phone on silent during performances.
- **Interesting Facts:** The festival hosts a mix of international and local performers, creating an event that's both highbrow and culturally enriching.

These Verona-inspired spots in Phuket create a perfect blend of history, art, and romance, ideal for visitors looking to connect with the legend of Romeo and Juliet.

Parma and Modena: Parmesan, Prosciutto, and Balsamic Vinegar

Northern Italy's culinary scene is a true reflection of its rich history and traditions, especially in the cities of Parma and Modena. These two places are the birthplace of some of the world's most iconic foods: Parmigiano-Reggiano (Parmesan cheese), Prosciutto di Parma (Parma ham), and Traditional Balsamic Vinegar of Modena. Each of these artisanal delights is more than just a product; they represent centuries of craftsmanship. Here's a guide to the best experiences centered around these iconic foods.

1. Parmesan Cheese – The King of Cheeses

Overview:

Parmesan is not just a cheese, it's an age-old tradition. Made from cow's milk, it's produced in the Parma region following strict methods that have been honed over hundreds of years. This cheese is a testament to Italian passion and precision in food craftsmanship.

Why Visit:

Visiting the Parmesan cheese factories in Parma gives you the chance to see how this iconic cheese is made, from curdling the milk to aging the cheese in storage rooms. It's a sensory experience that will leave you with a deeper appreciation for every grated flake you sprinkle over your pasta.

Location:

Various farms around Parma. One renowned place is *Caseificio San Pietro* (Address: Via San Pietro, 1, 43015 Noceto PR, Italy; GPS: 44.8383, 10.2465).

Website:http://www.parmigianoreggiano.com

Best Time to Visit:

The best months to visit are between April and October when the weather is pleasant for touring the countryside.

Admission Tickets:

Tours typically cost around €10-€20 per person, depending on the experience.

How to Get There:

The closest major city is Parma, about a 25-minute drive away. You can reach Parma by train from Milan or Bologna.

Opening Hours:

Tours generally operate from 9:00 AM to 6:00 PM. It's best to check with individual farms for availability.

Nearby Towns:

- Parma (Address: Piazza Garibaldi, 43121 Parma, Italy; GPS: 44.8015, 10.3279)
- Reggio Emilia (Address: Piazza Prampolini, 42121 Reggio Emilia, Italy; GPS: 44.6981, 10.6307)

What to Do & See:

Take a guided tour of the cheese production process. Watch the cheese being aged, and enjoy tastings paired with wine.

Nearby Restaurants & Attractions:

- *Osteria dei Mascalzoni* (Address: Via Mistrali, 23, 43100 Parma, Italy; GPS: 44.8015, 10.3281)
- *Teatro Farnese* (Address: Piazza Castello, 43121 Parma, Italy; GPS: 44.8043, 10.3274)

Photography Tips:

Capture the aging process in the dimly lit cellars, highlighting the texture of the cheese wheels.

Laws/Rules:
Be respectful of the farm's working environment; always follow the guide's instructions.

2. Prosciutto di Parma – The Ham of Tradition

Overview:
This sweet, delicate, dry-cured ham is a cornerstone of Italian cuisine, made from specially selected pigs raised in the Parma region. Its distinctive flavor comes from the traditional air-curing process, which can take up to 24 months.

Why Visit:

A tour of the Prosciutto di Parma factory lets you witness the meticulous curing process, often in picturesque ham cellars, where the ham is left to age naturally in the cool air of Parma.

Location:
Salumificio Conti (Address: Via Don Angelo Azzali, 26, 43030 Noceto PR, Italy; GPS: 44.8391, 10.2281).

Website:http://www.prosciuttodiparma.com

Best Time to Visit:

Spring and autumn are ideal, with fewer tourists and pleasant weather.

Admission Tickets:

Tours generally cost between €10-€25.

How to Get There:

Located 30 minutes from Parma by car or train.

Opening Hours:

Most factories open from 9:00 AM to 6:00 PM.

Nearby Towns:

- Parma (Address: Piazza Garibaldi, 43121 Parma, Italy; GPS: 44.8015, 10.3279)
- Langhirano (Address: Piazza della Pace, 43010 Langhirano PR, Italy; GPS: 44.6696, 10.1729)

What to Do & See:

Observe the detailed process of ham production, from salting to the final curing stages. Enjoy a tasting at the end.

Nearby Restaurants & Attractions:

- *Trattoria Ai Due Platani* (Address: Via Mazzini, 1, 43013 Langhirano PR, Italy; GPS: 44.6733, 10.1984)
- *Castello di Torrechiara* (Address: Via Castello, 1, 43010 Torrechiara PR, Italy; GPS: 44.6923, 10.1614)

Photography Tips:

Capture the ham hanging in cellars, the beautiful aging room, and close-ups of the curing process.

Laws/Rules:

Don't touch or disturb the products during your visit.

Overview:

This rich, tangy vinegar is made from a blend of cooked grape must and aged for years. Unlike the commercial versions, traditional Balsamic Vinegar of Modena is aged in wooden barrels, giving it a deep complexity.

Why Visit:

A tour of a balsamic vinegar producer provides a chance to explore centuries of tradition and craft, witnessing the vinegar being aged in barrel houses. You'll also sample different varieties, each with unique flavor profiles.

Location:
Acetaia Malpighi (Address: Via Riva, 5, 41015 Modena, Italy; GPS: 44.5517, 10.9875).

Website:http://www.acetaiamalpighi.com

Best Time to Visit:

Any time of year is perfect, but autumn offers a particularly charming atmosphere as the grape harvest season winds down.

Admission Tickets:

Prices typically range from €15-€30.

How to Get There:

The factory is about a 10-minute drive from Modena's city center.

Opening Hours:

Open from 9:00 AM to 5:00 PM.

Nearby Towns:

- Modena (Address: Piazza Grande, 41121 Modena, Italy; GPS: 44.6471, 10.9252)
- Carpi (Address: Piazza dei Martiri, 41012 Carpi MO, Italy; GPS: 44.7647, 10.8971)

What to Do & See:

Take a guided tour of the balsamic vinegar production process and end with a tasting.

Nearby Restaurants & Attractions:

- *Osteria Francescana* (Address: Via Stella, 22, 41121 Modena, Italy; GPS: 44.6474, 10.9269)
- *Duomo di Modena* (Address: Piazza Grande, 41121 Modena, Italy; GPS: 44.6478, 10.9258)

Photography Tips:

Capture the intricate wooden barrels and the gleaming dark vinegar.

Laws/Rules:
As with the other sites, always follow the guidelines to avoid contaminating or damaging the aging products.

Practical Information for Travelers:

- **Currency:** Euro (€)
- **Language:** Italian
- **Emergency Numbers:** 112 for general emergencies, 118 for medical emergencies

- **Weather:** Expect hot summers and cold winters, with spring and autumn being more temperate.

These three iconic products from Parma and Modena offer a true taste of Italy, steeped in history and tradition. Take time to savor the craftsmanship that has stood the test of time.

Genoa and Cinque Terre: Maritime Heritage and Coastal Beauty

Northern Italy is a region that speaks to the heart of any traveler. Among its gems, Genoa and Cinque Terre stand out as places where history, culture, and natural beauty meet. Genoa, the ancient maritime republic, offers a taste of Italy's past, while Cinque Terre's coastal villages offer views that seem to come straight out of a postcard. These two locations promise unforgettable experiences for visitors looking for history, beauty, and an authentic Italian atmosphere.

1. Genoa's Old Port

Overview:
Genoa's Old Port (Porto Antico) is the heart of the city's maritime legacy. Once a bustling commercial hub, today it's a vibrant area offering shopping, dining, and stunning views of the Ligurian Sea.

Why visit:

A stroll through Porto Antico is like stepping back in time, but with modern touches. This area is home to museums, the aquarium, and a great selection of restaurants, making it a lively and family-friendly stop.

Location:
Address: Piazza Caricamento, 16100 Genoa, Italy

GPS: 44.4061° N, 8.9185° E

Official Website:http://www.portoantico.it

Best time to visit:

Spring and fall are ideal, as the weather is pleasant and the crowds are thinner.

Admission:
Free to explore, but some attractions, like the aquarium, charge for entry.

How to get there:

By foot from Genoa city center or take bus lines 1, 18, or 36.

Hours:
Open daily, 24 hours for walking and sightseeing.

Closest town:

- Genoa
- Address: Genoa, Italy
- GPS: 44.4056° N, 8.9463° E

What to see and do:

Visit the Aquarium of Genoa, the largest in Italy, explore the maritime museums, or take a ride on the Bigo lift for panoramic views of the harbor.

Nearby restaurants:

- **Ristorante**   **La**   **Sailor**
  Address: Via al Porto Antico, 16128 Genoa, Italy
  GPS: 44.4054° N, 8.9182° E
- **Caffè**   **degli**   **Specchi**
  Address: Via San Lorenzo 61R, 16123 Genoa, Italy
  GPS: 44.4117° N, 8.9307° E

Photography tips:

Capture the sunset over the harbor and the old ships for that classic maritime shot.

Practical info:

Be aware that the area can get crowded, especially on weekends. Stick to the main walkways for a safer experience.

Interesting fact:

Genoa's Old Port was revitalized in the 1990s by renowned architect Renzo Piano, who brought the area back to life without losing its historical charm.

2. Cinque Terre: Monterosso al Mare

Overview:
Monterosso is the largest of the five villages that make up Cinque Terre, known for its beautiful beaches and vibrant old town.

Why visit:

If you're looking to relax on the beach and explore charming streets lined with colorful buildings, Monterosso is the perfect stop. It also has the region's largest selection of eateries and shops.

Location:

Address: Monterosso al Mare, 19016, La Spezia, Italy

GPS: 44.1693° N, 9.6175° E

Official Website:https://www.parconazionale5terre.it

Best time to visit:

May to October offers the best weather, though the summer months can get crowded.

Admission:
Free to explore, but there is a small fee for hiking paths between the villages.

How to get there:

Trains run regularly from La Spezia to Monterosso, or you can drive or take a ferry from neighboring towns.

Hours:
Monterosso is open year-round, though some businesses may close during winter.

Closest town:

- La Spezia
- Address: La Spezia, Italy
- GPS: 44.1023° N, 9.8243° E

What to see and do:

Relax at Fegina Beach, hike the Sentiero Azzurro trail, or wander through the old town and visit the Church of San Giovanni Battista.

Nearby restaurants:

- **Ristorante   Miky**
  Address: Via Fegina, 19016 Monterosso al Mare, Italy
  GPS: 44.1697° N, 9.6171° E
- **Trattoria   da   Oscar**
  Address: Via Roma 14, 19016 Monterosso al Mare, Italy
  GPS: 44.1714° N, 9.6183° E

Photography tips:

Capture the colorful buildings against the backdrop of the blue sea and sky.

Practical info:

The Cinque Terre Card is available for visitors and provides access to the trails and trains between villages.

Interesting fact:

Monterosso is home to the statue of Neptune, a beautiful bronze sculpture on the seafront.

Overview:

Vernazza is one of the most picturesque villages in Cinque Terre, perched on a cliff with a small, bustling harbor.

Why visit:

Known for its dramatic setting and beautiful harbor, Vernazza is ideal for a leisurely stroll through its narrow streets and a swim in the crystal-clear waters.

Location:

Address: Vernazza, 19018, La Spezia, Italy

GPS: 44.1072° N, 9.7002° E

Official Website:http://www.vernazzaturismo.com

Best time to visit:

Late spring and early autumn are the best times to enjoy the peaceful atmosphere.

Admission:
Free to wander, though some attractions charge an entry fee.

How to get there:

Train from La Spezia or boat from nearby Cinque Terre villages.

Hours:
Open year-round, but some businesses may close in winter.

Closest town:

- La Spezia
- Address: La Spezia, Italy
- GPS: 44.1023° N, 9.8243° E

What to see and do:

Visit the Church of Santa Margherita di Antiochia, enjoy a boat tour of the coast, or hike the Sentiero Rosso.

Nearby restaurants:

- **Ristorante Il Gambero Rosso**
  Address: Via Roma 1, 19018 Vernazza, Italy
  GPS: 44.1074° N, 9.7005° E
- **Belforte**
  Address: Via San Giovanni Battista, 19018 Vernazza, Italy
  GPS: 44.1070° N, 9.7003° E

Photography tips:

The harbor at sunset is one of the best photo opportunities in Italy.

Practical info:

The streets are steep and winding, so wear comfortable shoes.

Interesting fact:

Vernazza is the only village in Cinque Terre with a natural harbor.

By visiting Genoa's Old Port and the stunning villages of Cinque Terre, you'll experience a perfect blend of history, culture, and breathtaking scenery. Whether you're a history buff or simply looking to relax by the sea, these locations are sure to leave you with memories that will last a lifetime.

Turin: The Royal City of Chocolate, Cinema, and Shrouded Mysteries

Turin, located at the foot of the Alps, is a city that quietly pulsates with history, culture, and a touch of mystery. Whether you're here for its royal past, cinematic legacy, or rich chocolate history, this city offers much more than meets the eye. Here's a guide to the top six places to explore, where to go, what to see, and how to make the most of your visit.

1. Royal Palace of Turin

Overview

The Royal Palace of Turin is one of the most important historical sites in Italy. Once the residence of the House of Savoy, the palace stands as a testament to the grandeur of the Italian monarchy. Marvel at its opulent rooms, stunning gardens, and impressive artwork.

Why You Should Visit

For lovers of history and art, this royal residence provides a glimpse into the lavish life of Italy's monarchy. Don't miss the stunning Royal Gardens, offering a peaceful escape from the bustle of the city.

Location

Piazza Castello, 10122 Turin, Italy

GPS: 45.0702°   N,   7.6868°   E

Best Time to Visit

Spring and early fall are ideal, as the weather is pleasant, and the gardens are in full bloom.

Admission

- o   €15 (Adults)
- o   €2 (Students and under 18)

How to Get There

By foot from Piazza Castello, or take the tram (lines 4, 9, and 13).

Opening Hours

10:00 AM – 6:00 PM (Closed Mondays)

Closest Town

- o   Pinerolo, Italy
- o   Location: Piazza San Donato, 10064 Pinerolo, Italy
- o   GPS: 44.8841° N, 7.3276° E

What to Do and See

Explore the lavish rooms and learn about the royal history, including the chapel and the museum dedicated to the House of Savoy.

Nearby Restaurants & Attractions

- **Ristorante Del Cambio**
  Location: Piazza Carignano 2, 10123 Turin, Italy

GPS: 45.0704° N, 7.6885° E
Famous for traditional Piedmontese cuisine and historical charm.

- **Museo Egizio**
  Location: Via Accademia delle Scienze, 6, 10123 Turin, Italy
  GPS: 45.0705° N, 7.6789° E
  One of the most important Egyptian museums outside Egypt.

Photography Tips

Capture the intricate details of the palace's architecture. Early morning or late afternoon light provides beautiful shots of the gardens.

Practical Information

Wear comfortable shoes as there's a lot of walking involved, especially in the gardens.

2. Mole Antonelliana

Overview
This towering symbol of Turin is known for its impressive architecture and the National Museum of Cinema housed within. The panoramic views of the city from the top are unforgettable.

Why You Should Visit

For cinema enthusiasts and architecture lovers, the Mole Antonelliana offers an immersive experience with exhibits dedicated to the history of cinema. The view from the top is one of the best in the city.

Location

- Via Montebello, 20, 10124 Turin, Italy
- GPS: 45.0700° N, 7.6904° E
- https://www.moleantonelliana.it

Best Time to Visit

Morning visits are recommended to avoid crowds and get the clearest views of the city.

Admission

- €15 (Adults)
- €10 (Students)

How to Get There

The closest tram stop is "Mole Antonelliana" on line 15.

Opening Hours

10:00 AM – 8:00 PM (Closed on Mondays)

Closest Town

- Chieri, Italy
- Location: Piazza Cavour, 10023 Chieri, Italy
- GPS: 45.0099° N, 7.7555° E

What to Do and See

Explore the museum's fascinating collection of film history and ascend to the top for stunning views of the Alps.

Nearby Restaurants & Attractions

- **Eataly Torino Lingotto**
  Location: Via Nizza, 230, 10126 Turin, Italy
  GPS: 45.0354° N, 7.6767° E
  A food lover's paradise showcasing the best of Italian culinary delights.
- **Piazza Vittorio Veneto**
  Location: 10123 Turin, Italy
  GPS: 45.0703° N, 7.6882° E
  A lovely square near the river with cafes and a scenic view.

Photography Tips

The best photos are from the top, offering sweeping views of the city and the Alps.

Practical Information

Don't forget to check the weather forecast as fog can obscure the mountain views.

3. Egyptian Museum

Overview
Home to one of the most significant collections of Egyptian antiquities outside Egypt, this museum offers a deep dive into the ancient world with over 30,000 artifacts.

Why You Should Visit

History buffs and those intrigued by ancient cultures will find this museum fascinating. Its immersive exhibits bring ancient Egypt to life in the heart of Turin.

Location

- Via Accademia delle Scienze, 6, 10123 Turin, Italy
- GPS: 45.0705° N, 7.6789° E

Best Time to Visit

Visit during weekdays to avoid crowds.

Admission

- €15 (Adults)
- €10 (Students)

How to Get There

Accessible by foot from Piazza Castello.

Opening Hours

9:00 AM – 6:30 PM (Closed Mondays)

Closest Town

- Settimo Torinese, Italy
- Location: Piazza della Repubblica, 10036 Settimo Torinese, Italy
- GPS: 45.1156° N, 7.7863° E

What to Do and See

See mummies, statues, and hieroglyphs, and immerse yourself in the ancient rituals of Egypt.

Nearby Restaurants & Attractions

- **Caffè Mulassano**
  Location: Piazza Castello, 15, 10123 Turin, Italy
  GPS: 45.0701° N, 7.6850° E
  Historic café serving delicious pastries and coffee.
- **Parco del Valentino**
  Location: Corso Massimo d'Azeglio, 10126 Turin, Italy
  GPS: 45.0706° N, 7.6877° E
  A large public park perfect for a relaxing walk.

Photography Tips

Look for unique angles around the displays for intriguing shots of the statues and artifacts.

Practical Information

The museum can get busy, especially on weekends, so it's best to visit in the morning.

4. Turin's Chocolate Tour

Overview
A trip to Turin wouldn't be complete without experiencing its famous chocolate. The city has been making chocolate since the 16th century, and its chocolatiers are some of the finest in Italy.

Why You Should Visit

Taste the world-renowned Gianduiotto, a hazelnut and chocolate confection. Turin's historic cafés and chocolate shops offer a taste of Italian sweetness like no other.

Location

- Various locations around Turin
- https://www.turismotorino.org

Best Time to Visit

Year-round, though winter is especially cozy for enjoying chocolate.

Admission

Varies by location and tour packages.

How to Get There

Tours are walking tours, starting from various central locations.

Opening Hours

Tour times vary by package.

Closest Town

- Alba, Italy
- Location: Piazza Risorgimento, 12051 Alba, Italy
- GPS: 44.6897° N, 8.2064° E

What to Do and See

Sample the finest chocolates and learn about Turin's chocolate-making history.

Nearby Restaurants & Attractions

- **Cioccolateria Guido Gobino**
  Location: Via Lagrange, 1, 10123 Turin, Italy
  GPS: 45.0704° N, 7.6852° E

Photography Tips

Capture the intricate designs of the chocolate confections.

Practical Information

Check ahead for special events or chocolate festivals that might coincide with your visit.

5. Piazza Castello

Overview
This central square is home to some of Turin's most iconic buildings, including the Royal Palace and Palazzo Madama. It's the perfect spot to start your exploration of the city.

Why You Should Visit

The square is the beating heart of Turin and a great place to soak in the architecture and atmosphere of the city.

Location

- Piazza Castello, 10122 Turin, Italy
- GPS: 45.0705° N, 7.6875° E

Best Time to Visit

Anytime during the day, but particularly beautiful at sunset.

Admission: Free

How to Get There

Accessible by foot from most central locations.

Opening Hours

Always open.

Closest Town

- Rivoli, Italy
- Location: Piazza Martiri, 10098 Rivoli, Italy

Hours of Opening: Daily from 9:00 AM to 7:00 PM, closed on Mondays.

Closest Town

None, but located in central Turin.

What to Do and See

Explore the Royal Apartments, the Chapel of the Holy Shroud, and the beautiful gardens. The adjacent Museo Archeologico hosts fascinating Roman relics.

Best Nearby Restaurants & Attractions

- **Caffè al Bicerin**
  Location: Piazza della Consolata, 5, 10122 Turin, Italy
  GPS: 45.0700° N, 7.6878° E
  A historic café known for its signature drink, Bicerin, a rich mix of espresso, chocolate, and milk.

- **Piazza San Carlo**
  Location: Piazza San Carlo, 10121 Turin, Italy
  GPS: 45.0671° N, 7.6885° E
  Turin's main square, perfect for people-watching, with grand arcades and elegant cafés.

Photography   Tips
Capture the palace's magnificent baroque architecture from the gardens, especially at sunrise or sunset for the best light.

Laws/Rules
No flash photography inside the palace.

Practical   Information
Wear comfortable shoes as the palace grounds and museum require a fair amount of walking.

Interesting   Fact
The Royal Palace was the birthplace of the first King of Italy, Victor Emmanuel II.

6. Mole Antonelliana & National Cinema Museum

Overview
The Mole Antonelliana, one of the most iconic landmarks in Turin, now houses the National Cinema Museum. The building itself is a masterpiece of 19th-century architecture and offers panoramic views over the city from its top.

Why You Should Visit

A must-see for cinema buffs, the museum hosts interactive exhibits about the history of Italian and world cinema. Plus, the panoramic view from the top is not to be missed.

Location

- Via Montebello, 20, 10124 Turin, Italy
- GPS: 45.0703° N, 7.6866° E
- https://www.moleantonelliana.it

Best Time to Visit

Spring or early fall for fewer crowds and pleasant weather.

Admission

- €15 (Adults)
- €8 (Children and Students)

How to Get There

Easily accessible by tram (lines 13, 15, 4) or by foot from central Turin.

Hours of Opening

Daily from 9:00 AM to 8:00 PM.

Closest Town

Central Turin

What to Do and See

Visit the museum to explore cinema history, and don't miss the elevator ride up the Mole Antonelliana for a breathtaking view of the city and Alps.

Best Nearby Restaurants & Attractions

- **Ristorante del Cambio**
  Location: Piazza Carignano, 2, 10123 Turin, Italy
  GPS: 45.0706° N, 7.6869° E
  A historic restaurant known for traditional Piedmontese cuisine.
- **Piazza Carignano**
  Location: Piazza Carignano, 10123 Turin, Italy
  GPS: 45.0706° N, 7.6870° E
  A charming square with grand architecture and elegant cafés.

Photography Tips

The view from the top of Mole Antonelliana offers the best photo ops, especially during sunset.

Laws/Rules

No large bags or backpacks allowed in the museum.

Practical Information

The elevator to the top can be a bit crowded, so visit early in the day for a quieter experience.

Interesting Fact

The Mole Antonelliana was originally conceived as a synagogue and is named after its architect, Alessandro Antonelli.

Chapter 10: Crafting Your Northern Italy Itinerary

Planning your Northern Italy journey can be as exciting as the adventure itself. From the vibrant streets of Milan to the serene beauty of Lake Como and the historic allure of Verona, this guide offers carefully curated itineraries. Whether you have three, five, seven, or ten days, immerse yourself in the timeless magic of this region.

3-Day Highlights: Milan, Lake Como, and Verona

Northern Italy is a treasure trove of culture, landscapes, and history. Whether you're craving vibrant city life, serene lakeside escapes, or alpine adventures, this region caters to all interests. Here's a breakdown of itineraries to help you plan your perfect getaway.

If you're short on time, this quick itinerary provides an exciting overview of Northern Italy's gems.

Day 1: Milan

Start in Milan, Italy's fashion and design capital. Begin at the Duomo, an architectural marvel, then walk through the Galleria Vittorio Emanuele II for luxury shopping or just to admire the magnificent interiors. Don't miss Da Vinci's *The Last Supper* at Santa Maria delle Grazie. End your day with dinner in the trendy Brera district, known for its elegant restaurants and local charm.

Day 2: Lake Como

Take a day trip to Lake Como, just an hour from Milan. Board a ferry to explore picturesque lakeside towns like Bellagio and Varenna, where cobbled streets, cozy cafes, and lake views create a magical experience. Consider a villa tour, such as Villa Balbianello, for a touch of Italian opulence.

Day 3: Verona

Head to Verona, a city brimming with history. Walk across the medieval Ponte Pietra, visit Juliet's Balcony, and explore the Roman Arena, still used for performances today. Enjoy a hearty Veneto meal before concluding your short but impactful trip.

Estimated Budget:

- Accommodation: €200–€300
- Transport: €100
- Meals: €100–€150
- Activities: €80
  Total: €480–€630 per person

5-Day Exploration: Venice, Dolomites, and the Lakes

This plan balances iconic destinations with natural wonders.

Day 1-2: Venice

Begin in Venice, a city like no other. Wander through St. Mark's Square, visit the Doge's Palace, and ride a gondola down the Grand Canal. Spend your second day exploring the lesser-visited islands of Murano, known for its glassmaking, and Burano, famous for brightly painted houses.

Day 3: Dolomites

Head north to the Dolomites, a UNESCO World Heritage site. Base yourself in Cortina d'Ampezzo and enjoy a day of hiking or a leisurely cable car ride to panoramic viewpoints. This alpine region is breathtaking in both summer and winter.

Day 4: Lake Garda

Travel to Lake Garda, Italy's largest lake. Explore Sirmione, a charming town known for its Scaliger Castle and Roman ruins. Relax by the lake with gelato or take a boat ride to soak in the scenery.

Day 5: Return to Verona or Milan

Spend your last day revisiting Verona or returning to Milan for any sights you missed.

Estimated Budget:

- Accommodation: €350–€500
- Transport: €150
- Meals: €150–€200
- Activities: €100

- **Total: €750–€950 per person**

7-Day Journey: Cities, Cuisine, and Alpine Adventures

For a week-long trip, enjoy a mix of urban and rural experiences.

Day 1-2: Milan and Bergamo

Kick off your journey in Milan with its iconic landmarks. On Day 2, take a short trip to Bergamo, a city split into the ancient Città Alta and modern Città Bassa. Explore the medieval streets, Piazza Vecchia, and the views from the Venetian Walls.

Day 3-4: Lake Como and Lake Maggiore

Spend two days alternating between Lake Como and Lake Maggiore. In Como, indulge in lakeside dining and scenic walks. At Maggiore, visit Isola Bella and the opulent Borromean Palace.

Day 5-6: Dolomites

Drive or take a train to the Dolomites for outdoor activities like hiking or skiing, depending on the season. Relax in a mountain spa or try local dishes like polenta and speck.

Day 7: Venice

Conclude in Venice, where the unique streets and canals provide the perfect backdrop for your final day. Enjoy fresh seafood and a sunset view from a lesser-known spot like Fondamenta delle Zattere.

Estimated Budget:

- Accommodation: €500–€700
- Transport: €200
- Meals: €200–€250
- Activities: €150–€200

- **Total: €1,050–€1,350 per person**

10-Day Immersion: From Cultural Icons to Hidden Villages

For those with more time, this itinerary dives deep into Northern Italy's highlights and quieter corners.

Day 1-3: Milan, Lake Como, and Bergamo

Follow the highlights of the 3-day itinerary, but add a night in Bergamo to fully experience its atmosphere and cuisine.

Day 4-5: Venice and Surroundings

After exploring Venice, venture to the Prosecco Hills for wine tasting and peaceful landscapes.

Day 6-7: Dolomites and Bolzano

Spend two days hiking or skiing in the Dolomites. Include a visit to Bolzano, where Italian and Austrian influences blend beautifully. Explore the South Tyrol Museum of Archaeology to see Ötzi, the preserved Ice Age mummy.

Day 8: Parma and Modena

Head to Emilia-Romagna to savor culinary delights. Tour Parma's cheese factories or Modena's balsamic vinegar producers. Don't forget to try traditional tortellini or a glass of Lambrusco.

Day 9: Lake Garda

Relax by Lake Garda, exploring the charming towns dotting its shores. Treat yourself to a boat ride or visit the Gardaland amusement park if traveling with family.

Day 10: Verona

Wrap up in Verona, where Shakespearean romance and ancient history combine. Climb to Castel San Pietro for a panoramic view before heading home.

Estimated Budget:

- Accommodation: €900–€1,200
- Transport: €300
- Meals: €300–€400
- Activities: €250

- **Total: €1,750–€2,100 per person**

Tips for Planning

- **Transportation:** Trains are reliable and connect major cities. Renting a car is best for exploring the Dolomites and smaller towns.
- **Seasonal Considerations:** Summer is great for lakes and hiking, while winter attracts skiers to the Dolomites. Fall offers wine harvests and fewer crowds.
- **Accommodations:** Mix boutique hotels with agriturismi (farm stays) for a unique experience.

Northern Italy promises unforgettable experiences, whether you're spending three days or ten. With this guide, you'll craft a trip that suits your pace and interests while savoring all the region has to offer.

Chapter 11: Travel Tips for a Seamless Adventure

Planning a journey through Northern Italy can be an adventure to cherish, but a little preparation goes a long way. This chapter guides you through practical tips to make your trip smooth—from respecting local customs and staying safe to packing smart and traveling sustainably. Let's prepare for an unforgettable experience.

Customs and Etiquette: How to Blend In Like a Local

Blending in with the locals in Northern Italy requires an understanding of traditions and social nuances. It's not just about speaking Italian—it's about adopting the subtleties of the culture.

Dress Smartly: Italians value appearance and tend to dress with care, even for casual outings. Avoid overly casual attire like flip-flops or gym clothes when dining out or visiting public places. A tailored jacket or neat blouse can go a long way in making a good impression.

Dining Etiquette: Meals are treated with respect and savored slowly. Don't rush through courses or expect a quick coffee to go—espresso is meant to be enjoyed at the counter. Also, avoid asking for modifications to dishes unless absolutely necessary; it's seen as a slight to the chef's expertise.

Greetings and Interactions: When meeting someone, a firm handshake suffices in formal settings. Among friends, it's customary to exchange two light kisses on the cheeks, starting with the right cheek. Always greet with "Buongiorno" (good morning) or "Buonasera" (good evening), as greetings are an important part of politeness.

Punctuality and Timing: Northern Italians are generally more punctual than their southern counterparts. Arriving late to an appointment or dinner can be considered disrespectful.

Respect for Tradition: Be mindful when visiting churches or historical sites. Modest clothing is appreciated, and speaking in hushed tones shows respect for the environment.

Social Sensitivity: Italians value family and close friendships, so be patient when forming connections. A genuine interest in local customs and traditions will naturally build rapport.

By observing these unspoken rules, you'll not only avoid awkward moments but also feel more connected to the community.

Staying Safe and Healthy While Exploring

Exploring Northern Italy is an unforgettable experience, but ensuring your safety and health during your travels is essential. Here are some key tips to help you stay safe and enjoy all this beautiful region offers:

1. **Stay Hydrated**: Northern Italy's climate can be warm, especially in the summer. Always carry a water bottle and drink plenty to stay refreshed. Tap water is safe to drink in most places, so refill as needed.
2. **Secure Your Belongings**: Keep your valuables, like passports and wallets, in a secure place. Use a money belt or a zippered bag to avoid pickpocketing, especially in busy areas like Milan or Venice.
3. **Be Cautious with Food**: While Italy is known for its delicious cuisine, be cautious with street food, especially in tourist-heavy areas. Always eat at reputable places to avoid foodborne illnesses.

4. **Watch Out for Traffic**: Northern Italy's cities have busy streets and narrow alleys. Always look both ways when crossing, even if the pedestrian light is green, and be mindful of scooters and cyclists.
5. **Pack Properly**: Comfortable shoes are a must for exploring cobblestone streets, while layers will keep you prepared for changing weather. Bring a light jacket, as evenings can be cool, even in summer.
6. **Know Emergency Numbers**: In case of an emergency, Italy's emergency number is 112. It's a good idea to have a basic understanding of Italian phrases related to medical or safety issues.
7. **Health Insurance**: Before you travel, make sure you have travel insurance that covers health emergencies. Many pharmacies in Italy can assist with minor ailments, but knowing where the nearest hospital or clinic is can be helpful.

By keeping these tips in mind, you can ensure a safe, healthy, and enjoyable journey through Northern Italy's captivating landscapes and cities.

Packing Essentials for Northern Italy's Seasons and Activities

Northern Italy is a region of contrasts, offering everything from majestic mountains and serene lakes to bustling cities and charming villages. Packing for this region depends heavily on the time of year and the activities you plan to enjoy. To help you prepare, here's a practical guide to packing essentials tailored to Northern Italy's seasons and activities.

Spring (March to May):

Spring brings mild temperatures, but unpredictable weather calls for layers. Pack light sweaters, long-sleeve shirts, and a water-resistant jacket. A pair of comfortable walking shoes is a must for exploring cities like Milan or Verona. Don't forget a compact umbrella, as showers are common.

Summer (June to August):

Summers can get warm, especially in cities. Lightweight and breathable fabrics like linen and cotton are your best friends. Include shorts, dresses, and short-sleeve shirts for daytime and a light jacket for cooler evenings by the lakes. If you're planning to visit coastal areas like Liguria, add swimwear, a wide-brimmed hat, and sunglasses.

Autumn (September to November):

Autumn in Northern Italy is crisp and colorful. Warm layers are key, including sweaters, scarves, and a thicker jacket for evenings. Waterproof footwear is essential if you'll be walking on cobbled streets during rainy days. Add gloves and a hat if you're heading to the mountains, where temperatures drop faster.

Winter (December to February):

Winter can vary depending on your location. For skiing in the Alps, pack insulated jackets, thermal layers, gloves, and snow boots. If you're staying in cities, opt for a wool coat, warm sweaters, and boots suitable for walking on icy streets. A scarf and hat are great for keeping warm during outdoor excursions.

Activity-Specific Items

- **Hiking and Nature Walks:** Comfortable hiking boots, moisture-wicking socks, a daypack, and reusable water bottles are essentials. Consider packing trekking poles if you're exploring mountain trails.
- **Cultural and City Exploration:** Smart-casual clothing works well for museums, restaurants, or opera nights. Don't forget a lightweight scarf for cathedrals or religious sites where modest dress is appreciated.
- **Skiing and Snowboarding:** Ski goggles, helmets, and weather-appropriate gloves should top your list. Renting larger equipment like skis or snowboards is often more convenient than carrying them.
- **Wine Tours and Countryside Visits:** Neutral-tone outfits and sturdy shoes are great for vineyard tours. If you're visiting during harvest season, a light jacket and a small tote for souvenirs or wine bottles can come in handy.

General Must-Haves

- **Electronics:** Bring a universal adapter, especially if you're coming from outside Europe. A portable charger is essential for long days exploring.
- **Toiletries:** While most items are available locally, pack any personal essentials, especially if you have specific skincare needs.
- **Documents:** Keep a travel folder with your passport, travel insurance, and copies of any reservations. Having these both digitally and physically is wise.

- Always check the weather forecast before you leave. Northern Italy's microclimates can vary significantly even within a short distance.
- Leave space in your suitcase for items you may pick up, like local wines, artisanal goods, or clothing from renowned fashion houses.
- Pack light to make room for souvenirs and to navigate trains and buses easily.

Northern Italy invites travelers to enjoy its seasons in comfort and style. With a little preparation, you'll be ready to experience the beauty and charm that this region is known for, no matter when you visit.

Eco-Friendly Travel: Supporting Local Communities and Sustainability

Northern Italy offers travelers the opportunity to enjoy its natural beauty and cultural heritage while making conscious choices that benefit the environment and local communities. Here's how you can make your trip meaningful and sustainable:

1. **Choose Local Accommodations**

   Opt for family-run guesthouses or eco-certified hotels. Many establishments are committed to reducing waste and supporting local traditions, giving you a genuine connection to the area.

2. **Support Artisans and Farmers**
   Explore local markets in towns like Parma and Modena, where you can buy handmade crafts, organic produce, and regional delicacies. This not only ensures authenticity but also uplifts small businesses.

3. **Eco-Friendly Transportation**

Northern Italy's efficient train network makes it easy to travel with minimal environmental impact. Consider cycling in scenic areas like Lake Garda or walking through the vineyards of Barolo for a slower, immersive experience.

4. **Visit Responsible Wineries and Farms**

   Discover wineries and agriturismos (farm stays) that use sustainable farming methods. These spots often welcome visitors to learn about eco-conscious practices while enjoying locally sourced food and wine.

5. **Respect Natural Spaces**

   When hiking in the Dolomites or visiting serene lakes, stick to marked trails and leave no trace. Carry reusable water bottles and avoid single-use plastics to minimize waste.

6. **Engage in Community-Based Tourism**

   Participate in workshops or guided tours led by locals. Activities like pasta-making classes in Bologna or traditional mask painting in Venice allow you to learn while contributing directly to the community.

Travel in Northern Italy can be both enriching and sustainable when choices align with respect for the environment and its people. Thoughtful planning ensures your visit leaves a positive footprint.

Conclusion: Northern Italy – Where Every Journey Begins Again

As your time in Northern Italy draws to a close, it's impossible not to reflect on the profound experiences this region offers. From the soaring peaks of the Dolomites to the shimmering waters of Lake Como, Northern Italy doesn't just leave an impression—it lingers in your thoughts, calling you to return. Every corner of this land seems to echo with stories, inviting you to add your own to its endless chapters.

Reflections on Northern Italy's Timeless Beauty

Northern Italy feels like a timeless masterpiece—every element thoughtfully placed, every view a scene etched in memory. Its cities buzz with life, its countryside offers moments of pure stillness, and its lakes and mountains seem to defy the boundaries of what is real and what feels like a dream. Beyond the landmarks and landscapes, it's the simple things that stay with you: the aroma of freshly brewed espresso in a quiet piazza, the laughter of locals sharing stories at a family-owned trattoria, and the golden light that graces the hills at sunset.

Why Northern Italy Will Call You Back

Northern Italy isn't the kind of place you visit once and check off your list. It's the kind of place that finds its way into your heart and stays there, whispering to you in quiet moments to come back. Perhaps it's the light in Venice, shifting with the tides, or the quiet trails in the Alps that urge you to explore further. Maybe it's the warmth of the people, the vibrancy of the culture, or the unshakable feeling that there's always more to uncover.

As your journey concludes, remember this: Northern Italy doesn't say goodbye. It merely pauses, leaving its doors open for when you're ready to return. And when you do, it will feel like picking up a story right where you left off—familiar yet new, comforting yet exciting. After all, in Northern Italy, every journey begins again.

Made in the USA
Las Vegas, NV
23 December 2024